A Troubleshooting Guide for Writers

D0039481

Seventh Edition

A Troubleshooting Guide for Writers

STRATEGIES AND PROCESS

Barbara Fine Clouse

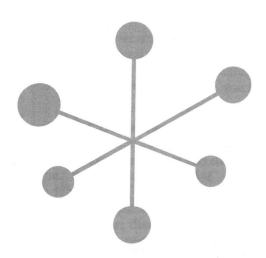

The **McGraw·Hill** Companies

A TROUBLESHOOTING GUIDE FOR WRITERS: STRATEGIES AND PROCESS, SEVENTH EDITION

ISBN: 978-0-07-340591-9
MHID: 0-07-340591-4

Vice President & Editor-in-Chief: *Michael Ryan*
Vice President & Director Specialized Publishing: *Janice M. Roerig-Blong*
Publisher: *David Patterson*
Sponsoring Editor: *Jessica Cannavo*
Marketing Manager: *Kevin Colleary*
Senior Project Manager: *Joyce Watters*
Design Coordinator: *Brenda A. Rolwes*
Cover Design: *Studio Montage. St. Louis, Missouri*
Buyer: *Sandy Ludovissy*
Media Project Manager: *Sridevi Palani*
Compositor: *Aptara®, Inc.*
Typeface: *9.75/12 Meridian*
Printer: *RR Donnelley, Crawfordsville*

Library of Congress Cataloging-in-Publication Data

Clouse, Barbara Fine.
  A troubleshooting guide for writers : strategies and process / Barbara Fine Clouse.—7th ed.
     p. cm.
  Includes index.
  ISBN-13: 978-0-07-340591-9 (acid-free paper)
  ISBN-10: 0-07-340591-4 (acid-free paper)
  1. English language—Rhetoric.   2. English language—Grammar. 3. Report writing.   I. Title.
PE1408.C5378 2012
808'.042—dc22   2011037345

www.mhhe.com

For Violet Rae Clouse

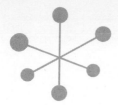

Table of Contents

Chapter Five
"I'm Having Trouble with My Introduction." 48

Preface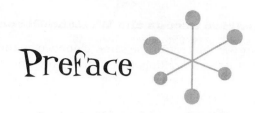

A Troubleshooting Guide for Writers: Strategies and Process is a compendium of strategies for handling all aspects of writing, from idea generation through editing. It is based on the belief that people write better when they discover procedures that work well for them.

Goals

The many writing strategies in *A Troubleshooting Guide for Writers* serve two important purposes:

- They provide a range of strategies for writers to sample as they work to develop successful writing processes.
- They help writers when they get stuck by providing specific strategies for solving their writing problems.

Features

The features of *A Troubleshooting Guide for Writers* make it an efficient reference for solving writing problems and for discovering effective writing procedures.

New: Additional Helpful Strategies

Nineteen new strategies (for a total of 332) make *A Troubleshooting Guide* more useful than ever! With so many helpful procedures, all users should find ways to solve problems and improve their writing processes.

Clear, Jargon-Free Prose Written in a Conversational Style

So the book can be a ready reference both in and out of the classroom, explanations are concise and written in a supportive, inviting style.

Organization across the Writing Process

Writers can use the text in the same sequence as their writing. Part I treats pre-writing; Part II treats drafting; Part III treats revising; Part IV treats editing.

Chapters Structured as Responses to Questions and Comments Voiced by Student Writers

Students can find what they need faster because chapter titles echo their own language and concerns.

An Overview of the Writing Process and Essay Structure

The Introduction contains information on the stages of writing, audience, purpose, and essay structure, with an emphasis on writing a thesis.

<u>New</u>: A Student Essay to Serve as a Model

The introduction includes a new, annotated student essay to illustrate points made about essay structure.

A Focus on Collaboration

In addition to offering strategies to help students incorporate peer response into their revision processes, Chapter 11 includes information on how students can provide genuinely useful feedback to other writers.

<u>New</u>: An Expanded Discussion of Research and Using Sources

Part V, which focuses on finding and using source material and which includes an annotated student paper with sources, has been expanded to include:

- More sample MLA and APA models.
- More on finding and evaluating sources.
- An expanded and updated list of online references and search tools.
- More on using high quality sources.
- A new discussion of reading sources strategically.
- A new discussion of incorporating notes in the outline.

Plagiarism Alerts

Explanations for avoiding intentional and unintentional plagiarism appear at strategic points throughout the book.

New: Updated Examples

Examples have been updated to freshen the text.

An Emphasis on Composing at the Computer

Since students routinely use computers, strategies for composing at the computer have been integrated into the main text.

Strategies for Multilingual Students

Appendix A describes strategies particularly helpful to students who use English as a second or third language.

Strategies for In-Class Writing

Appendix B includes strategies for in-class writing and for taking essay examinations.

❋ A NOTE TO STUDENTS

Pretend for a moment that you play tennis and that you are having trouble with your baseline shots. A coach, noticing your problem, might suggest that you drop your hip a little. Now pretend that you are a runner, and you are having trouble improving your time in the 1,600-meter race. In this case, your coach might suggest that you swing your arms more and pretend a giant hand is on your back pushing you along. That's what coaches do: They make suggestions to help you solve problems that arise as a natural part of learning to do something better.

As you work to become a better writer, think of this book as one of your coaches. If you encounter a problem, look to this book for one or more suggestions for solving that problem.

❋ HOW TO USE THIS BOOK FOR BEST RESULTS

- Read over the table of contents so you know what this book covers. Notice that most of the chapters are titled with a remark often spoken by a struggling writer.
- If you get stuck, return to the table of contents and find the remark that best expresses the problem you are having. Turn to the chapter titled with that remark.

- Quickly read the chapter (it will be short). Several strategies for solving your writing problem will be explained. Select one of the strategies and give it a try. If it works, great. If not, try another—and another—until you solve your problem. (If none of the procedures works, speak to your instructor or a writing center tutor.)
- If you are not having any problems but want to discover more effective or efficient procedures, read through the book and mark the procedures to try the next time you write.

Of course, this book is not your only coach. Your classroom teacher is the best coach of all, and your classmates and the tutors in the writing center are also good sources of information. So if you have a problem, you can also talk to one of these people to get suggestions for overcoming the obstacle. Ask them what procedures they follow, and try some of them to see if they work for you too.

Acknowledgments

I am grateful to Nancy Huebner, Jessica Cannavo, and Andrea Edwards for their support and expert guidance. In addition, I owe much to the sound counsel of the following reviewers, whose insights inform this book:

Sheryl Bundy
Moraine Valley Community College

Mary Corey
Baker College

Scott Empric
Housatonic Community College

Michele LaPorta
Long Beach City College

John Minchin
California Southern University

Connie Warner
Baker College

Julie Whitlow
Salem State University

Special thanks go to to the following reviewers of past and current editions who contributed strategies:

Charlyne Berens, University of Nebraska at Lincoln, for the "substitute he and him" strategy in Chapter 20

Sheryl Bundy, Moraine Valley Community College, for the "highlight paragraph beginnings and endings" strategy in Chapter 12

Scott Empric, Housatonic Community College, for the "discuss early versions of the thesis" strategy in Chapter 2

John Minchin, California Southern University, for the "tape a spelling list to your computer" strategy in Chapter 27

Juanita Smart, Clarion University of Pennsylvania, for the "echo conclusion" strategy in Chapter 7

Finally, to my understanding husband, Denny, and to my children, Greg and Jeff, I offer thanks for the support and for the room of my own.

A Troubleshooting Guide for Writers is also available in an electronic format from CourseSmart. CourseSmart is a new way to find and buy e-textbooks. At Course-Smart you can save up to 50 percent off the cost of a print textbook, reduce your impact on the environment, and gain access to powerful Web tools for learning. CourseSmart has the largest selection of e-textbooks available anywhere, offering thousands of the most commonly adopted textbooks from a wide variety of higher education publishers. CourseSmart e-textbooks are available in one standard online reader with full text search, notes and highlighting, and e-mail tools for sharing notes between classmates. For further details contact your sales representative or go to www.coursesmart.com.

A Troubleshooting Guide for Writers

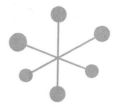

Myths about Writing

AN INTRODUCTION

People say many things about writing. Some of what they say is true, but some of it is not. Can you tell the difference?

TEST YOURSELF: Myth or Fact?

Which of the following statements are facts, and which are myths? (The next section will supply the answers, but don't peek.)

Writers are born, not made.

"Good" writers write fast.

Writers should wait for inspiration.

"Good" writers rarely struggle.

"Good" writers get it right the first time.

Outlining is very time-consuming.

The longer the words, the better they are.

Revising is reading over a draft and fixing spelling and punctuation.

After drafting, "good" writers look for their grammar mistakes right away.

(continued)

There is only one way to write.

An essay has no identifiable parts.

Introductions should be written first.

A well-stated point does not require proof.

After making their last point, writers should just stop.

Sentence fragments are always short.

Run-ons and comma splices are always long.

Use a comma wherever you pause in speech.

Capitalize a word to emphasize it.

There are no rules to explain English spelling.

The longer the writing, the better it is.

DON'T BELIEVE EVERYTHING YOU HEAR

Much of what you hear about writing just isn't true, including the statements in the box above—every one of those statements is a common myth about writing. If you are surprised to learn that these statements are untrue, read the chapters indicated below for accurate information.

Myth	Accurate Information
Writers are born, not made.	Introduction
"Good" writers write fast.	Chapters 9–16
Writers should wait for inspiration.	Chapter 1
"Good" writers rarely struggle.	Introduction
"Good" writers get it right the first time.	Chapters 4–16
Outlining is very time-consuming.	Chapter 3
The longer the words, the better they are.	Chapter 8
Revising is reading over a draft and fixing spelling and punctuation.	Chapters 10–11
After drafting, "good" writers look for their grammar mistakes right away.	Introduction
There is only one way to write.	Chapters 1–16

How to Become a Better Writer

MYTH: Writers are born, not made.

"I'm a terrible writer." Students say that all the time, and maybe you have said it yourself. If so, you are probably wrong. More likely, you are not as good a writer as you could be—or would like to be—but now you have the chance to become a better writer, even an excellent one.

Perhaps you think you can't be a good writer because you weren't *born* a good writer. Again, you are mistaken, for you can *learn* to be a good writer. Becoming a better writer is like becoming a better swimmer, piano player, or dancer. In all these cases, you can work to improve a skill. As you work to improve your writing skills, think about the following habits of highly successful writers.

7 HABITS OF HIGHLY SUCCESSFUL WRITERS

1. **Be patient.** Improving a skill takes time. Just as perfecting a foul shot takes a basketball player time and practice, so too does improving your writing. If you expect too much too soon, you will become frustrated. Look for slow, steady progress rather than dramatic, overnight improvement.

2. **Expect to get stuck.** Everyone does, even experienced, professional writers. Writer's block and dead ends are all part of writing, so do not think there is something wrong with you if you have some trouble. Consult this text, your instructor, other experienced writers, and/or a writing center tutor when you get stuck. When you solve the problem, tuck the solution away for future reference, so the same problem does not plague you over and over again.

3. **Remember that writing is really rewriting.** Experienced writers work and rework drafts several times. With each revision, know that you are acting like an experienced writer.

4. **Talk to other writers.** Find out what they do when they write, and try some of their procedures. Form a network with your classmates and other writers for support and suggestions.

5. **Study the responses to your writing.** What does your instructor say about your writing? What do your classmates say when they read your drafts? What do people in the writing center say? Reader response is valuable to a writer. By paying attention to this response and working to improve areas where readers see weaknesses, you can improve more quickly. If you do not understand a response or if you do not know how to make a change, ask for help.

6. **Read, read, read.** Read every day—the newspaper, newsmagazines, short stories, crime novels, anything that interests you. Notice how other writers handle introductions, conclusions, supporting detail, and transitions. Look up unfamiliar words, notice sentence structure, and observe punctuation. The more you read, the more you learn about the nature of language, and the faster your writing will improve. Furthermore, frequent reading makes you more knowledgeable, so you have more ideas for your writing.

7. **Do not fear mistakes.** They are a natural part of learning. Take risks; try things out. If you make mistakes, embrace them as opportunities to learn. If you are afraid of making a mistake, you will never try; if you never try, you will never grow. Connect your mistakes to your writing procedures. Decide which procedures work well for you and which do not. Then consult this text and your instructor for procedures to replace ones that did not work. For example, maybe idea generation goes well for you, but revision does not. That means you need to discover new revision procedures. When your procedures work better, your writing will improve.

Understand That Writing Is a Process

MYTH: "Good" writers write fast.

Very few worthwhile endeavors are accomplished quickly, and writing is no different. Successful writers typically engage in a number of activities, and doing so takes time. These activities are

1. Prewriting
2. Drafting
3. Revising
4. Editing

Writers do not always move in a straight line from prewriting to drafting to revising to editing. Instead, they often double back before going forward. For example, while drafting you may think of a new idea to add, so you have left drafting and doubled back to prewriting. While editing, you may think of a better way to phrase an idea, so you have left editing and doubled back to revising. Never consider any stage of the process "done" and behind you. Always stand ready to respond to a good idea.

Now let's consider what each stage of writing involves.

Prewriting

MYTH: Writers should wait for inspiration.

If you sit around waiting for inspiration, you may never get anything written; inspiration does not occur often enough for writers to depend on it. In fact, inspiration occurs so rarely that writers must develop other ways to get ideas. Collectively, the procedures for coming up with ideas in the absence of inspiration are called **prewriting.** The term *prewriting* is used because these procedures come before writing the first draft.

Chapters 1–3 describe procedures for coming up with ideas to write about and for discovering ways to order those ideas.

Drafting

MYTH: "Good" writers get it right the first time.

Once writers generate enough ideas during prewriting to serve as a departure point, they make their first attempt at writing those ideas. This part of the writing process is **drafting.** Typically, the first draft is very rough, which is why it is so often called the **rough draft.** The rough draft provides raw material that can be shaped and refined in the next stages of the writing process.

Chapters 4–8 describe drafting procedures.

Revising

MYTH: Revising is reading over a draft and fixing spelling and punctuation.

When **revising,** writers rework the raw material of the draft to get it in shape. This reworking is a time-consuming, difficult part of the process. It requires the writer to refine the content so that it is clear, so that points are adequately supported, and so that ideas are expressed in the best way possible and in the best order possible.

Chapters 9–16 describe revising procedures.

Editing

MYTH: After drafting, "good" writers look for their grammar mistakes right away.

Because experienced readers expect your writing to be free of errors, you must **edit** to find and eliminate mistakes. However, many writers hunt for errors too soon, before they have revised for content and effective expression. Save editing for the end of the process.

Chapters 17–27 describe editing procedures.

Develop Your Own Writing Process

MYTH: There is only one way to write.

Although we have been discussing "the" writing process, there really is no single correct process. Instead, writers develop procedures that work well for them, so every successful writer can have a different, successful process. As you use this book and work to become a better writer, try different strategies for prewriting, drafting, revising, and editing. Some of these procedures will work well for you, and some will not. Continue sampling until you have effective strategies for handling all the stages of writing, and at that point you will have discovered your own successful process.

Be Aware of Your Purpose

Everything you write has a purpose. Even something as simple as a grocery list is written for a purpose: to make sure you don't forget to buy everything you need. The fact is, if you don't have a reason for writing, why bother?

Four common purposes for writing are

- To relate experience
- To inform
- To persuade
- To entertain

The first reason for writing is to **relate experience,** perhaps to express your feelings about the experience or reflect upon it. For example, if you interviewed to be a lab assistant in the biology department, afterward you might write a friend an e-mail about the experience and how nervous you were. People enjoy sharing experiences because doing so helps them connect with others. You might also write in your journal to reflect on what happened and evaluate your interview. Written reflection is valuable as a way to understand events.

Another reason for writing is to **inform,** perhaps to increase the reader's knowledge, establish a record, or provide help. For example, a magazine article about cholesterol can increase a reader's understanding of how this substance affects the body. The proceedings of government agencies recorded into documents serve as a permanent history. The owner's manual for a Blu-ray player explains how to operate the device so that the owner can use it properly. We need informational writing to communicate important knowledge with others and to preserve significant facts.

A third reason for writing is to **persuade** a reader to think or act a particular way. For example, you might write a letter to the editor of your campus newspaper to convince students to vote for a particular student government candidate. Or you might write a letter to convince a store manager to refund your money for a defective product you purchased. People are always trying to influence each other, and persuasive writing is one way they exert that influence.

The last reason for writing is to **entertain.** Short stories, romance novels, and humorous newspaper columns, for example, are written to entertain. Without such creative writing, we would lose an important pleasure, and our lives would be diminished.

Finally, writers often combine purposes. For example, you might write a description of your favorite fishing spot both to share your fishing experience there *and* to entertain your reader.

You must be aware of your purpose for writing because purpose affects what you write and how you write it. Say you are writing about discovering mice in the apartment you just rented. Notice how different the writings become when your purpose changes:

To relate experience	The writing might tell how upset you are about the discovery of the mice.
To inform	The writing might explain what happens when a dwelling has mice in it, or it could explain how one rids a dwelling of mice.
To persuade	The writing might give reasons your landlord should refund your rent and deposit because of the mice, or it might give reasons why people should have apartments inspected before signing a rental contract.
To entertain	The writing might be a funny story about what it is like living with mice.

Think about Your Reader

Your **audience** (the person or people who will read your writing) affects what you say and how you say it. For example, say that you need to borrow $100 to get through the month because you did not live within your budget. If you were e-mailing a close friend to request the loan, your writing would be relaxed and informal. You might not even explain why you have come up short or when you will repay the money. Your writing might be something like this:

To...	Dale Frazier
Cc...	
Subject:	help!

Hey, Dale –

I hate to do this to you, but I need a hundred bucks fast – never mind why. I'll get it back to you as soon as I can.

Lee

If you were writing a note to your parents, you would be a little more formal and forthcoming about why you need the money and how you will pay it back:

My cell phone bill was higher than I expected, so I'm short of money this month. I'm really sorry—I've learned my lesson about text messaging. I plan to work overtime three days next week, so I know I can repay the loan after my next paycheck.

Now consider a letter asking your boss to advance you $100. For this audience, your writing would be the most formal of all. It could look like the letter on page 9.

As you can see, your reader's situation affects what you write. For example, assume you are writing to convince your reader that a longer school year is a good idea. If your audience includes working mothers, you might mention that a longer school year will cut down on child care hassles. However, if your audience includes teenagers, this argument would mean little. Instead, you might note that they would be more competitive when they apply for admission into college.

One way to gear your writing to your audience is to complete a reader profile like the one explained on pages 73–74.

NOTE: Perhaps you are thinking that if you are in a writing class your audience will be your writing instructor. Yes, but writing teachers can assume the identities of different audiences, so you can practice writing for a range of readers.

450 Granada Avenue
Truesdale, OH 44512
January 14, 2011

Ms. Marian Mattura, General Manager
The Campus Diner
88501 Lane Avenue
Truesdale, OH 44520

Dear Ms. Mattura:

I wish to request a $100 advance on my salary for next month. I
hope the fact that I have been a reliable employee at the Campus
Diner for two years and the fact that I have never asked for an
advance in the past will persuade you to grant my request.

Ms. Mattura, I am already scheduled to work overtime three
days next week, so I am certain I will have no trouble repaying
this loan. I am also certain I will never need to ask for an
advance again, because I now understand the importance
of sticking to a budget.

Thank you very much for considering my request.

Sincerely,

Lee

Lee Coombs

TEST YOURSELF: Find the Intersection of Audience and Purpose

Two pieces of writing that have the same purpose will be very different if
written for different audiences. Consider the recruitment letters sent out by
your college admissions office. A letter aimed at recruiting a star high school
athlete may highlight one aspect of your college, while a letter aimed at a
prospective theater major may highlight a different aspect. Similarly, pieces
written for the same audience but with different purposes will also be different.
Consider two letters sent out by your school's alumni office to recent graduates.
A letter inviting the graduates to join the alumni association will be very
different from one soliciting a contribution to the school.

Three Writing Tasks Assume that you borrowed your brother's car and that while it was parked someone sideswiped it, causing extensive damage. Now assume you have three writing tasks ahead of you:

1. Leaving your brother a note explaining what happened to the car.

2. Writing your parents to explain what happened so you can borrow money to have the car fixed.

3. Writing your friend who attends another school to tell that person what happened.

How will these three pieces of writing differ? Explain how the audience and purpose are responsible for those differences.

Know What an Essay Is

MYTH: An essay has no identifiable parts.

Pause for a moment and think about the forms people use for their writing: letters, memos, diary and journal entries, e-mail, Web pages, blogs, message board postings, chat room comments, Facebook, Twitter, lab reports, book reports, résumés, newspaper and magazine articles, editorials, advertisements, brochures, even flyers tacked up on telephone poles—and that's not all of them. In college, however, the most frequently used form is the **essay**—a brief writing composed of several paragraphs, all relating to a single topic.

Although there is no single correct essay format, you can learn one very serviceable structure that will work in most writing situations. An essay with this structure has three parts:

- The introduction
- The body paragraphs
- The conclusion

The Introduction

MYTH: Introductions should be written first.

The opening paragraph or paragraphs of an essay are the **introduction.** The introduction creates interest in the essay, so readers want to read on. Have you ever started a magazine article, read a paragraph or so, and moved on to another article without finishing? If so, the introduction failed to stimulate your interest. You don't have to write your introduction before the rest of your paper. Sometimes the best introductions are written last.

Chapter 5 explains strategies for writing introductions that stimulate reader interest.

The Thesis

In addition to creating interest in the essay, the introduction often includes a **thesis,** which is the statement of the essay's topic and your assertion about that topic, like this:

Thesis	Network news broadcasts do not adequately inform the public.
Topic	Network news broadcasts
Assertion	They do an inadequate job of informing the public.

A good thesis presents an idea worth writing about—something disputed or in need of explanation.

Acceptable thesis	Although everyone agrees that children must be adequately cared for, this country does not properly regulate day care centers.
Explanation	The thesis idea is debatable and in need of explanation.
Unacceptable thesis	Children must be adequately cared for.
Explanation	No one will disagree with the thesis idea, so why bother writing about it?
Acceptable thesis	Rose Lewin, my grandmother, is a woman of courage and determination.
Explanation	The thesis idea requires explanation.
Unacceptable thesis	Rose Lewin is my grandmother.
Explanation	The thesis idea is a statement of fact that requires no explanation and needs no debate.

Chapter 2 explains strategies for writing acceptable thesis statements.

To give you an idea of how an introduction can stimulate interest and present the thesis, here is an introduction taken from the essay on pages 16–18.

The writer stimulates interest with a vivid description of serious problems we currently face.

We seem to be living in an era with a heightened sense of our own impending doom. The polar ice caps are melting before our eyes, causing floods in some regions, drought in others and extreme storms in yet others. We are losing many species every year due to human activity and habitat loss, and many more are in danger of extinction. If that's not bad enough, our oceans are filling up with junk,

The thesis
is underlined
as a study aid.

whirling around in vortexes the size of Texas, made mostly of plastic waste like discarded bottles, grocery bags, and fishing net. Not surprisingly, food and energy prices have soared, contributing to political uprisings in the Middle East and economic malaise in the United States and Europe. Any one of these problems would be daunting enough in its own right, but together they are practically overwhelming. Fortunately, one possible solution—human population control—addresses every one of these issues at the root. <u>We should make zero population growth a world-wide goal</u>.

The Body Paragraphs

MYTH: A well-stated point does not require proof.

Do you believe everything you read? Of course not, and your audience doesn't either. That's why your reader will not believe your thesis is true unless you *prove* that it is. Does your thesis state that schools should teach conflict resolution? Then you have to provide solid reasons why doing so is a good idea. Does your thesis state that high-protein weight-loss diets can be dangerous? Then you must explain how the diets can be harmful. Does your thesis state that the new education building is an eyesore? Then you need to describe the unattractive features of the building. And that is where the body paragraphs come in. The **body paragraphs** present the ideas that prove or explain your thesis, so your reader will accept its truth.

Body paragraphs typically have two parts:

- The topic sentence
- The supporting details

The **topic sentence** tells what point the paragraph makes to prove or explain the thesis. The **supporting details** are all the ideas that develop the topic sentence's point. To help you recognize the two parts of a body paragraph, examine these two body paragraphs, written to prove or explain the thesis, "We should make zero population growth a world-wide goal." (The topic sentences are underlined as a study aid.)

The topic sentence
presents one point
to explain or
prove the thesis.

<u>In reality, current levels of population growth are already unsustainable</u>. For one thing, we are not adequately feeding the people already on the planet. Far too many children starve to

The supporting details develop the point stated in the topic sentence.

death each year while others suffer from debilitating diseases related to malnutrition and vitamin deficiencies. Ironically, even in the Western countries where food is plentiful, diets for the poor are calorie rich but nutrient poor because junk food is cheaper than nutritious food. With climate change, rising energy and food prices, and increasing competition for world resources from developing countries eager to transition to Western lifestyles, our relative food security in the developing world is set to change dramatically.

The supporting details develop the point stated in the topic sentence

In truth, the future looks grim. Our population continues to grow. We are depleting our resources (water, cropland, fossil fuels, forests, and fisheries) faster than we can replace them given our current technologies, borrowing from the past when we burn fossil fuels to produce our food and borrowing from the future when we clear cut pristine rainforests or deplete existing food stocks to the point of no return. At our current numbers, we are creating waste and other pollutants faster than they can be reduced to nontoxic levels through normal natural processes. To put it in medical terms, we have reached the limits of healthy growth and have entered a malignant phase where additional growth of any kind threatens vital organ systems and potentially the health of the planet as a whole. Unless we take action now, there will be millions more of us to feed by midcentury, and no resources available to do it.

The topic sentence presents one point to explain or prove the thesis.

The Topic Sentence

Often, as the first body paragraph above illustrates, the topic sentence comes at or near the beginning of the paragraph. Sometimes, as the second body paragraph above illustrates, the topic sentence comes at or near the end of the paragraph. When you place the topic sentence first or nearly first, you give your reader an up-front statement of the point you will develop in support of the thesis, and then you go on to provide supporting details to prove that point. When you place your topic sentence last or nearly last, your supporting details provide specific evidence that leads to the conclusion stated in the topic sentence.

The Supporting Details

Your supporting details must be **adequate,** which means you must have enough of them to prove or explain the thesis and each topic sentence to your reader's satisfaction. To appreciate the importance of adequate detail, read the following body paragraph, which does *not* have adequate detail.

> In reality, current levels of population growth are already unsustainable. We are heading for serious trouble. For one thing, we are not adequately feeding the people already on the planet. With climate change and other problems, our relative food security in the developing world is set to change dramatically.

Now reread the first sample body paragraph on pages 12–13 to see how much more convincing the paragraph is because of the more substantial supporting details.

Writers have many strategies for providing adequate detail, including describing, telling a story, giving examples, explaining causes and/or effects, showing similarities and/or differences, and showing how something is made or done.

Chapter 6 tells more about strategies for providing adequate supporting details.

In addition to being adequate, supporting details must be **relevant,** which means they must be directly related to both the thesis and the topic sentence of the paragraph they appear in. For example, a paragraph with the topic sentence, "Zero population growth will reduce the poverty rate in the United States" should not include detail about how ZPG will improve the health of people all over the world. This detail is not relevant to the topic sentence, and including it will sidetrack your reader.

Finally, body paragraphs and supporting details should be presented in a logical order, perhaps one of the following:

- <u>In order of importance</u> (from the least significant to the most significant point)—An essay arguing against restricting immigration might begin with the least compelling reasons and move on to the most compelling reasons.

- <u>In time order</u> (from the first event to the last event)—A story can begin with the first event and proceed in sequence to the last event.

- <u>From general to specific</u> (from a general statement to specific examples) or <u>from specific to general</u> (from specific examples to general statements)—An essay explaining the value of a liberal arts education can first state that a liberal arts education makes a person versatile and then give specific examples of that versatility. Or it can first give examples of the benefits of a liberal arts education and then conclude with the statement that the education makes a person versatile.

- <u>In order across space</u> (from near to far, front to back, left to right, and so forth)—A real estate brochure describing a house can arrange details from room to room.

- In a problem–solution order (a statement of a problem followed by an explanation of a solution)—A magazine article about Americans' lack of physical fitness might first explain the problem and then offer suggestions for solving it.
- In a cause-and-effect order (an explanation of why an event occurs followed by an explanation of the results of that event)—A research paper about the Nixon presidency could give the causes of the Watergate scandal and go on to note the effects of the scandal on American politics.

The Conclusion

> **MYTH:** After making their last point, writers should just stop.

The end of an essay is the **conclusion.** Conclusions are important because final impressions are important. To realize this, think back to the last movie or television show you watched that ended badly. Remember how let down you felt? You do not want to leave your reader feeling let down, because a negative final impression can undermine the effectiveness of the entire essay. Instead, provide closure, a sense of comfortable completeness—like that provided in this conclusion from "Make Zero Population Growth a world-wide Goal" an essay that appears next.

> Historically, we've managed population explosion through exploration and conquest. But we are one world now, and there are no new frontiers. We know now that population collapse can be swift and brutal, and if we don't take action, nature will. If we really care about human rights, the future of the planet, and our species, we should take immediate action to limit our numbers. Zero population growth should be a world-wide goal.

Chapter 7 explains strategies for writing conclusions.

 **A SAMPLE ESSAY**

The sample paragraphs in the preceding sections were taken from the essay that follows. (The thesis and topic sentences are underlined as a study aid.)

Make Zero Population Growth a World-Wide Goal

Stacey Sperling

[1] We seem to be living in an era with a heightened sense of our own impending doom. The polar ice caps are melting before our eyes, causing floods in some regions, drought in others, and extreme storms in yet others. We are losing many species every year due to human activity and habitat loss, and many more are in danger of extinction. If that's not bad enough, our oceans are filling up with junk, whirling around in vortexes the size of Texas, made mostly of plastic waste like discarded bottles, grocery bags, and fishing net. Not surprisingly, food and energy prices have soared, contributing to political uprisings in the Middle East and economic malaise in the United States and Europe. Any one of these problems would be daunting enough in its own right, but together they are practically overwhelming. Fortunately, one possible solution—human population control—addresses every one of these issues at the root. We should make zero population growth a world-wide goal.

[2] Zero population growth (ZPG) sounds a little scary, but it doesn't mean none of us will ever be allowed to have children. It simply means using existing birth control methods (preferably *not* abortion, infanticide, or forced sterilizations) on a *voluntary* basis to prevent a net increase in the overall population. In the developing world where people tend to live longer lives, the optimal rate of reproduction is often said to be about two children per woman, while in the developing world, where mortality rates are higher, it might be three or more, depending on local conditions. That means ZPG is a flexible goal, subject to ongoing adjustment and review.

[3] In reality, current levels of population growth are already unsustainable. For one thing, we are not adequately feeding the people already on the planet. Far too many children starve to death each year while others suffer from debilitating diseases related to malnutrition and vitamin deficiencies. Ironically, even in the western countries where food is plentiful, diets for the poor are calorie rich but nutrient poor because junk food is cheaper than nutritious food. With climate change, rising energy and food prices, and increasing competition for world resources from developing countries eager to transition to Western lifestyles, our relative food security in the developing world is set to change dramatically.

Margin notes:

The last sentence is the thesis. The material before the thesis stimulates interest.

The topic sentence is underlined. The supporting details explain what zero population growth is.

The topic sentence is underlined. The supporting details explain the need for ZPG.

The topic sentence is underlined. The supporting details ZPG.

[4]In truth, the future looks grim. Our population continues to grow. We are depleting our resources (water, cropland, fossil fuels, forests, and fisheries) faster than we can replace them given our current technologies, borrowing from the past when we burn fossil fuels to produce our food and borrowing from the future when we clear cut pristine rainforests or deplete existing food stocks to the point of no return. At our current numbers, we are creating waste and other pollutants faster than they can be reduced to nontoxic levels through normal natural processes. To put it in medical terms, we have reached the limits of healthy growth and have entered a malignant phase where additional growth of any kind threatens vital organ systems and potentially the health of the planet as a whole. Unless we take action now, there will be millions more of us to feed by midcentury, and no resources available to do it.

The topic sentence is underlined. The supporting details mention and refute an opposing argument.

[5]Despite the dire consequences of population growth, some people say that ZPG is too drastic a measure, and we should find another way. Certainly, we need innovative need innovative technologies to address the problem. However, creation and implementation of new technologies takes time. For now, we already have the technology necessary to manage human population growth (a wide variety of proven birth control methods), and we know it works.

The topic sentence is underlined. The supporting details are an example.

[6]China's one-child policy, which has been in effect since 1978, is a model we can learn from. Chinese officials made the one-child policy a matter of law, implemented public awareness campaigns, and used local officials to monitor and enforce the policy through the imposition of heavy fines for violations. China's authoritative central government approach would be difficult, if not impossible, to implement in Western countries, where reproductive self-determination is regarded as a basic human right, but that doesn't mean Western countries can't learn from China's example. Zero population growth would actually be a less drastic goal than China's one-child policy, which sets the ideal birth rate below the total number of deaths. Western countries could encourage zero population growth through an entirely voluntary program by providing tax breaks and other incentives like paid college tuition. They could easily follow China's example and conduct public message campaigns to publicize those benefits. An incentive-based system would also be less likely to foster some of the unintended consequences China experienced in the early years of the program like abortion, infanticide, gender imbalances, and underreporting of births.

The topic sentence is underlined. The supporting details give additional benefits of ZPG.

[7]Zero population growth has additional benefits beyond simply eradicating hunger and environmental degradation. Countries that voluntarily limit their population growth are less crowded, experience less poverty, and crime, and have their healthcare institutions better able to provide care to mothers and their children than their overcrowded and stressed counterparts. Women who delay childbearing until later years (a major cornerstone of China's one-child program) are more likely to receive an education, more likely to survive childbirth, and more likely to raise their children into productive adult lives. And when women and children survive more reliably, their families are more willing to embrace family planning voluntarily in the interest of a more stable, higher quality life, establishing a virtuous, more sustainable cycle of development.

The conclusion provides closure by explaining the consequences of ignoring the thesis idea and by repeating that thesis idea.

[8]Historically, we've managed population explosion through exploration and conquest. But we are one world now, and there are no new frontiers. We know now that population collapse can be swift and brutal, and if we don't take action, nature will. If we really care about human rights, the future of the planet, and our species, we should take immediate action to limit our numbers. Zero population growth should be a world-wide goal.

TEST YOURSELF: Identify Essay Parts

As you have just read, essays often have an introduction, body paragraphs, and conclusion. Look at three editorials in your local newspaper and answer the following questions about each one:

1. Is there a separate introduction? If so, which paragraph(s) forms the introduction? What do you think of that introduction? Why?
2. If there is no separate introduction, should there be? Why or why not?
3. Do the body paragraphs do a good job of proving the writer's points? Explain.
4. Is there a separate conclusion? If so, does it create a strong final impression? Explain.
5. If there is no separate conclusion, should there be? Explain.

PART I

A Troubleshooting Guide to Prewriting

Has this happened to you? You stare at the blank page or screen, trying to squeeze out ideas, but nothing occurs to you. If so, you have experienced writer's block. Or you write a bit, wad up the paper or hit the delete key, and start again, but the same process repeats itself over and over. This experience is also writer's block. You can banish writer's block with the prewriting strategies in this section. (**Prewriting** refers to discovering ideas to write about.)

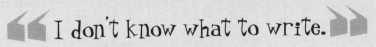

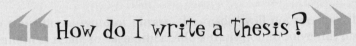 I don't know what to write.

Have you tried these?

❑ Freewriting (p. 21) ❑ Brainstorming (p. 25)

How do I write a thesis?

Have you tried these?

❑ Limiting your topic (p. 32) ❑ Using specific words (p. 32)

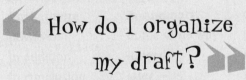 How do I organize
my draft?

Have you tried these?

❑ Checking your thesis (p. 34) ❑ Constructing an outline
map (p. 38)

CHAPTER ONE

"I Don't Know What to Write."

The terror of the blank page! No, it's not a movie coming soon to a theater near you. It's the fear writers experience when they cannot think of anything to write. Sure, some writers are zapped by the lightning bolt of inspiration, and idea after idea comes tumbling forth. However, inspiration is fickle and cannot be counted on to show up just because you have a paper due on Friday. If inspiration fails you, develop ideas on your own with the **idea generation techniques** described in this chapter.

FREEWRITE

With **freewriting,** you write to discover ideas to write about. It works like this: Sit in a quiet spot and write nonstop—either at the computer or with pen and paper—for about 10 minutes. Record every idea that occurs to you, no matter how silly or irrelevant it seems, and do not stop for any reason. If you run out of ideas, write the days of the week, names of your family members, even "I don't know what to write." In short, write *anything*—even wild or silly statements. Soon new thoughts will strike you, and you can write them. Do not evaluate anything or censor yourself. Do not worry about grammar, spelling, or neatness. Just write ideas the best you can.

Here is a freewriting to discover ideas for an essay about Twitter. Notice that the writer wrote ideas as they flowed and did not worry about correctness

People love or hate Twitter but it is here to stay. It has both good and bad aspects. On the good side is that people can stay in touch easy and let each other know what they are doing at any given moment. Friends and loved ones can stay in touch. Politicains use Twitter to let people know about their views so I guess you could say it helps democracy. You can't say much in detail though because a tweet is only 140 characters at the most. So I'm not sure if that's good or not.

Twitter may have it's benefits but sometimes the stuff on it is stupid. I want to connect with friends but I don't care that they are stopping in Starbucks now or on the way to do their laundry. It can be really important in an emergency like when someone lets their family know they are ok after a tornado. Hmm, what else? I can't think of anything. Oh, advertisers use it to let people know about their products, I guess that's good. And you can reconnect with people like high school friends you lost track of. What else? What else? What else? It can be addicting which is really a problem. Especially for college students.

The freewriting unearthed a number of ideas about the effects of Twitter. The writer can develop one or more of these ideas into an essay.

WRITE BLINDFOLDED

If you like to compose at the computer, turn the monitor off or turn the brightness dial down so your screen is dark, and freewrite. The dark screen may keep you from censoring yourself and encourage a freer flow of thought. After 10 minutes, restore your screen. You will probably have lots of typos, but they don't matter. You can still detect the seeds of usable ideas.

USE LOOPING

With **looping,** you explore a topic in more depth by doing a second and sometimes a third freewriting. For example, the previous freewriting on the effects of Twitter yielded the idea about Twitter becoming addictive. To use looping, you would freewrite on this topic. That second "loop" may yield enough material, or you may freewrite a third loop on an idea that emerged in the second loop. Taken together, all the freewriting loops can unearth considerable material.

TRY CLUSTERING

Clustering lets you see at a glance how ideas relate to one another. To cluster, write in the middle of a page a subject area you want to think about. Then draw a circle around the subject, so you have something that looks like this:

Next, as you think of ideas, connect them to the central circle:

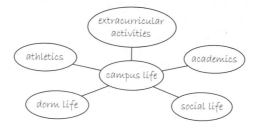

As more ideas occur to you, connect them to the appropriate circles:

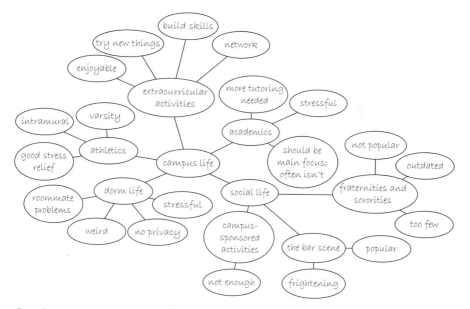

Continue writing ideas and joining them to circles until you can think of nothing else. Then study your clustering to see if one particular circle with its connecting circles gives you enough to begin a draft. For example, this portion of the previous clustering might serve as a departure point for a draft about the benefits of extracurricular activities:

If this clustering does not yield enough ideas for a draft, cluster again to expand the branches:

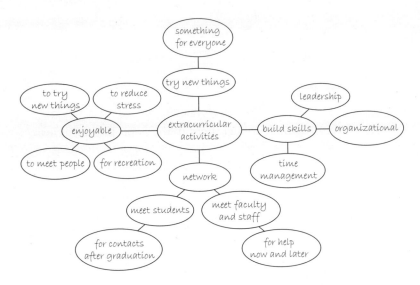

WRITE A LIST

At the computer or with pen and paper, list ideas that occur to you. Do not censor yourself. Even if you are sure an idea is terrible, write it anyway because it may prompt you to think of another, more useful idea. Here is an idea generation list for an essay about the effects of being cut from the basketball team:

felt rejected

was embarrassed

disappointed my father

got teased

felt inadequate

gave up basketball forever

decided to go out for cross-country

lost my best friend, who was busy with the team

Next, review your list and cross out or delete ideas you do not want to use and add new ideas that occur to you. If you number or arrange the ideas in the list in the order you want to treat them in your draft, you have a scratch outline.

Sometimes you may want to write a second list focusing on only one of the points in your first list. For example, a second list focusing on "lost my best friend, who was busy with the team" could look like this:

Cal had no time for me

practiced every day

couldn't go out at night because of curfew

socialized with his teammates

wouldn't play sports with me because of fear of injuries

BRAINSTORM

To **brainstorm** for ideas, ask yourself questions about your topic. Sometimes the question that offers up the most is the simple question "Why?" In addition, you can ask the following questions:

Why did it happen?	What is it similar to?
How did it happen?	What is it different from?
Who was involved?	What are its physical characteristics?
When did it happen?	Why is it important?
Where did it happen?	Who would care about it?
Could it happen again?	What causes it?
What does it mean?	What are its effects?
How does it work?	What is it related to?
Why does this matter to me?	What examples are there?
Why does this matter to my reader?	How can it be explained?
Why is it true?	What controversies are associated with it?

EXAMINE YOUR TOPIC FROM DIFFERENT ANGLES

If you have a broad subject area you want to write about, but you are not sure how to limit the subject, try viewing it from different angles. Asking yourself the following questions can show you how to approach your topic from different perspectives:

1. **How can I describe my subject?** What does it look, smell, taste, sound, and feel like? What are its parts, its color, its size, its shape, and so on?
2. **How can I compare and contrast my subject?** What is it like, and what is it different from? Are the similarities and differences important?
3. **What do I associate my subject with?** What does it make people think of? What is it related to? What does it develop from or lead to?
4. **How can I analyze my subject?** How is it broken down? How does it work? What is it made of? Why is it important?

5. **How can I apply my subject?** What is it good for? Who would find it useful? When is it useful? Does it have social, economic, or political value?

6. **What arguments accompany my subject?** What are the reasons for it? What are the reasons against it? Who is for it? Who is against it? Is it right or wrong? Good or bad? How does it affect society?

Use Questionnaires

Learning what other people think can lend perspective and stimulate your thinking. To discover what others think, develop a questionnaire for people to complete. This is not a scientific instrument; it is just something to prime your own idea pump. For example, say you want to write about the movie rating system. You could develop the following questionnaire for some students, faculty, family, and friends:

1. What do you think of the current movie rating system that uses the designations G, PG, PG-13, R, and NC-17?

2. Why do you think the way you do?

3. What could be done to improve the system?

4. What aspects of the current system should remain the same? Why?

Your questionnaire should not include too many questions, or people will not bother with it. Nor should you use the answers *instead* of your own thinking; the answers are meant to stimulate your own thinking. Finally, question at least five people, so you get a useful number of responses.

Write a Blog Entry

Writing a blog about your preliminary ideas serves two purposes. First, the act of writing can clarify your thinking and help you develop enough ideas to begin a first draft. Additionally, readers who respond to your blog can stimulate your thinking and contribute thoughts that become departure points for a draft.

Write an Exploratory Draft

You may not know what you want to say until you say it. Sit down and force yourself to write on your topic for about half an hour without worrying about how good the material is. The result will be an exploratory draft, a few pages of material reflecting what you currently know. An exploratory draft may yield a thought or two that you can pursue with one of the idea generation techniques in this chapter, or it may yield enough for you to try an outline or rough draft. Remember that your goal is not to produce a first draft of your essay; it is to discover one or more ideas for a departure point.

✳ RELATE THE TOPIC TO YOUR OWN EXPERIENCE

Relate the topic to your own experiences, so you can write about what you know. For example, if you have been asked to write about modern technology, remember all the trouble your smart phone caused you, and write an essay about how these devices can be more trouble than they are worth. If you have been asked to write about the American educational system, think about your child care hassles and argue that your college should have a day care center.

✳ FIND A FRESH ANGLE

Look for a fresh approach to your topic. For example, if you are writing about the stress that college students experience, consider something other than the familiar "reasons for the stress" or "ways to cope with stress." Perhaps you could write about the positive aspects of stress.

✳ TALK INTO A RECORDER

Forget writing and try talking. Have a conversation with yourself about your topic by speaking all your thoughts into a recorder. Do not censor yourself; just talk about whatever occurs to you. When you run out of ideas, play back the recording. When you hear a good idea, write it down.

✳ COMMUNICATE WITH OTHER PEOPLE

In person, by e-mail, or on a social networking site, discuss your writing topic with friends and relatives. They may be able to suggest ideas.

✳ WRITE A POEM

Sometimes changing formats can help, so instead of trying to write an essay, write a poem about your topic. Then study it for ideas you can shape and develop in essay form.

✳ WRITE ABOUT YOUR BLOCK

Write about why you can't write. Explain how you feel, what is keeping you from getting ideas, and what you would write if you could. This writing can catapult you beyond the block to productive idea generation.

PUT YOUR WRITING ON THE BACK BURNER

Give your ideas an incubation period. Go about your normal routine with your writing topic on the back burner, and think about your topic from time to time throughout the day. Many writers get their best ideas while walking the dog, washing the car, sitting in a traffic jam, or cleaning the house. If an idea strikes while you are in the middle of something, stop and write it down so you do not forget it.

IDENTIFY YOUR PURPOSE AND AUDIENCE

You may have trouble thinking of ideas if you have not clarified your purpose and audience (see pages 6–9). Responding to the following can help:

1. **To identify your purpose:**
   a. What feelings, ideas, or experiences can I relate to my reader?
   b. Of what can I inform my reader?
   c. Of what can I persuade my reader?
   d. In what way can I entertain my reader?

2. **To identify your audience:**
   a. Who could learn something from my writing?
   b. Who would enjoy reading about my topic?
   c. Who could be influenced to think or act a certain way?
   d. Who is interested in my topic or would find it important?
   e. Who needs to hear what I have to say?

KEEP A JOURNAL

Buy a full-size spiral notebook for keeping a journal or set up a computer file. A journal is not a diary because it is not a record of your daily activities. Instead, it is an account of your thoughts and reactions to events. For example, if you feel compassion for a blind person you met, describe your feelings. If you are anxious about an upcoming event, explain why you are concerned.

A journal is also a good place to think things through in writing. Do you have a problem? Explore the issues in your journal, and you may achieve new insights. In addition, if you are working on a writing project, a journal is an ideal place to try out an approach to part of the draft or tinker with a revision. A journal is also an excellent place to respond to what goes on in your classes: Summarize class notes, respond to reading assignments, and react to lectures to help learn course material.

Because your journal is meant for you and not for a reader, you do not need to revise or edit anything. Just write your ideas down any way that suits you. Later, if you are looking for a writing topic, review your journal for ideas.

Set aside at least 15 minutes every day to write in your journal. If you have trouble thinking of what to write, try one of the following suggestions:

1. Write about something that angers you, pleases you, or frustrates you.
2. Describe the ideal college education.
3. Write about some change you would like to make in yourself.
4. Look at a newspaper and respond to a headline.
5. Write about someone you admire.
6. Describe your life as you would like it to be in five years.
7. Tell about one thing the world should do without.
8. Record a vivid childhood memory.
9. Describe the best and worst features of your school.
10. Describe one piece of legislation you wish you could draft. Explain how it would improve the world.

Combine Techniques

Combine techniques any way you like. You can begin with freewriting and then brainstorm. Or you can talk into a recorder and then list. Experiment until you find the combination of techniques that works the best.

Develop Your Own Writing Topic

1. Try freewriting (see page 21). Begin something like this: "I need a writing topic. Maybe I could write about . . . "
2. Try clustering (page 22). Begin by placing one of these subjects in a circle in the center of the page: education, athletics, friendship, television, movies, family, automobiles, teenagers, memories, technology, the environment.
3. Consult your journal for topic ideas (see page 28).
4. Fill in the blanks in the following sentences:
    a. I'll never forget the time I _____.
    b. The best (or worst) thing about _____ is _____.
    c. My most embarrassing (or proudest) moment occurred when _____ _____.
    d. I wish I could change _____.
    e. _____ is the most _____ I know.
    f. The best way to _____ is _____.
    g. Few people understand the true meaning of _____.
    h. What this country needs is _____.

     i. Without _____, life would be very
       different.

     j. Few people understand the differences between _____ and

       _____.

     k. _____ and _____ are more alike than people
       realize.

Filling in the blanks in these sentences will not give you ready-to-use topics, but the completed sentences will *suggest* topics. For example, consider this completed sentence d:

I wish I could change the way public education is funded in this state.

This sentence could lead to the following topic:

Rather than using the property tax, this state should finance public education with an increased income tax.

5. Make a list of questions or problems, and use one of them as a departure point for additional idea generation. For example, your list could include some of the following:

     a. Do nice people really finish last?

     b. Why do women wear makeup when men don't?

     c. Is it too late to stop global warming?

     d. Why do so few people vote?

     e. Why are violent movies so popular?

6. Skim magazines and newspapers for ideas. An article on the Olympics could prompt you to write that the government should subsidize athletics. You can also browse electronic news sites, newspapers, and magazines, like one of these:

Google News: http://news.google.com

Reuters News Service: www.reuters.com

A national newspaper: www.usatoday.com

Links to magazines and newspapers: www.refdesk.com

PLAGIARISM ALERT

Plagiarism is a serious form of academic dishonesty that occurs if you intentionally or unintentionally pass off someone else's words or ideas as your own. When you use the Internet to find ideas, never download material and paste it into your paper so it appears to be your original thoughts. If you *do* use information, facts, opinions, or statistics from the Internet, be sure to give credit according to the conventions explained in Chapter 29.

CHAPTER TWO

"How Do I Write a Thesis?"

You know in your own mind what your essay is about, but that is not enough. You need to convey that idea to your reader in a clear, appealing way, and that's where your **thesis** comes in. Your thesis is the statement of your essay's focus (see page 11), and it frequently appears in your opening paragraph—the **introduction** (see page 10). Because your thesis guides the course of your essay, it must be crafted with care.

STUDY YOUR IDEA GENERATION MATERIAL

You may be tempted to base your thesis on the point for which you generated the most ideas, but that point may not be your best choice. Perhaps you have too much material for the length you are working with, or perhaps that point holds little interest for your reader. Study your idea generation material carefully with your reader in mind before deciding on your thesis idea.

DISCUSS EARLY VERSIONS OF YOUR THESIS WITH OTHERS

In person, on the phone, with e-mail, on Twitter, or on Facebook, share early versions of your thesis with other people to get their reactions. Ask them whether they would like to read an essay with the thesis you have written—and why or why not. Ask for suggestions for shaping your topic, making your assertion more specific, and finding language to create interest.

WRITE A TWO-PART THESIS

One part of your thesis should give the topic you are discussing, and the other part should note your assertion about that topic. In the following examples, the topics are underlined once, and the assertions are underlined twice:

The television ratings system does not serve the purpose it was intended to serve.

The federal government should outlaw Internet gambling.

Although textbooks cost a great deal of money, they are one of the best bargains in education.

Teachers should not get preferential parking on this campus.

✳ NOTE THE MAIN POINTS YOU WILL MAKE IN YOUR ESSAY

In addition to noting your topic and your assertion about that topic, your thesis can indicate the main points you will cover in your body paragraphs (although it does not have to do this). In the following example, the designated main points are underlined:

Year-round schools are a good idea because children would not forget material over long summer breaks, child care would not be a problem for working parents, and a greater number of elective courses could be offered.

✳ LIMIT YOUR THESIS TO SOMETHING MANAGEABLE

Your thesis should include just one topic, and that topic should not cover too much territory. Your thesis should also include just one assertion. If you include more than one topic, a very broad topic, or more than one assertion, you will have to write too much for a standard essay. Or you will be forced into a superficial discussion.

More than one topic	To revitalize the city, tax incentives should be offered to new businesses, and more parking should be offered downtown.
Better (one topic)	To revitalize the city, tax incentives should be offered to new businesses.
Better (one topic)	To revitalize the city, more parking should be offered downtown.
More than one assertion	Voters would be less apathetic if campaign finance laws were changed, and if candidates debated more often.
Better (one assertion)	Voters would be less apathetic if campaign finance laws were changed.
Better (one assertion)	Voters would be less apathetic if candidates debated more often.
Too broad	The American political system needs to be overhauled.
Better	The electoral college is no longer a sensible way to elect a president.

✳ EXPRESS YOUR ASSERTION IN SPECIFIC WORDS

Words like *good, nice, awesome, bad,* and *interesting* are too vague to give your reader a clear indication of your assertion, so opt for more specific words.

Vague	Jennifer Juarez makes a <u>good</u> candidate for city council.
Better	Jennifer Juarez is a qualified candidate for city council because of her extensive political background.
Vague	New York's Metropolitan Museum is an <u>awesome</u> place.
Better	Because of the number and variety of its holdings, New York's Metropolitan Museum is a national treasure.

✳ AVOID FACTUAL STATEMENTS

If your thesis is a statement of indisputable fact, your essay will have nowhere to go.

Factual statement	The zoning board must decide whether to approve a housing development on Route 193.
Better	The zoning board should approve the housing development on Route 193.

✳ AVOID ANNOUNCING YOUR INTENTIONS

Announcements like "This essay will show," "In the next paragraphs I will explain," and "My purpose is to prove" are reserved for scientific and technical papers.

Announcement	The purpose of this paper is to show why state lotteries are harmful to the average person.
Better	State lotteries are harmful to the average person.

✳ CONSIDER YOUR THESIS TO BE TENTATIVE

Write your thesis the best way you can, and don't worry if it isn't perfect yet. You will be able to improve it later, during revising.

✳ FILL IN THE BLANKS

Fill in the blanks in one of these sentences for a tentative thesis that you can improve later:

My topic is _____, and my assertion is _____.

The main idea I want my reader to understand is _____.

✳ RETURN TO IDEA GENERATION

If you have tried everything and cannot come up with a tentative thesis, you may not have enough ideas to begin after all. Return to idea generation, and try again.

CHAPTER THREE

"How Do I Get My Ideas to Fit Together?"

Okay, so you've come up with good ideas, and now you need to get your ideas to hang together in a coherent whole. The strategies in this chapter can help.

CHECK YOUR THESIS

Your thesis tells what your essay is about. (See Chapter 2.) If your ideas do not come together, check your thesis as explained here:

1. **Be sure you *have* a thesis.** Can you point to a specific sentence (or two) that expresses the focus of your writing? If not, your ideas may be nothing more than a collection of loosely related thoughts that seem confused because they do not develop one central focus.

2. **Be sure your thesis expresses an idea worthy of discussion,** something that is disputed or something in need of explanation. For more on this point, see page 11.

3. **Be sure your thesis does not take in too much territory,** or you will be forced to bring in too many ideas, which can create disorder.

Thesis covering too much territory	High school was a traumatic experience.
Acceptable thesis	My first high school track meet was a traumatic experience.

The first thesis requires the writer to cover events spanning four years—a great deal for one essay. The second thesis sets up a more reasonable goal—covering the events of one afternoon.

✳ Use Colored Markers or Fonts

List the ideas you have generated, and then use different colored markers to underline or highlight the ideas that relate to each other. The color will give you a visual map: All the green ideas will be discussed together, all the blue, all the red, and so on. Ideas without color may work well for your introduction or conclusion. Or perhaps you need to generate ideas to develop those points. If you like to compose at the computer, change the colors of your fonts to group your ideas.

✳ Write a Scratch Outline

To write a scratch outline, list your ideas and then number them in the order you will write them in your draft. If you compose at the computer, you can turn your idea generation list into a scratch outline by deleting ideas you do not want to use, adding new ideas that occur to you, and then using the copy and paste functions to arrange ideas in the order you will write them. A scratch outline can be made quickly and is useful for brief, uncomplicated writings. For longer, more complex pieces, you may want to use one of the outlining techniques explained next.

✳ Construct an Outline Tree

An outline tree provides a visual representation of how your ideas relate to each other. To construct a tree, write your thesis on the page:

A refundable deposit should be added to the price of products in glass containers.

Next, branch your main ideas off from your thesis idea:

Then branch supporting ideas off from your main ideas:

The outline tree shows you how ideas relate to each other so that when you draft, you are not skipping randomly from one idea to another.

❋ COMPLETE AN OUTLINE WORKSHEET

With an outline worksheet, you can plan your draft in a fair amount of detail without the roman numerals, letters, and numbers of a formal outline. Copy the form on page 37, and fill in the blanks with words and phrases that indicate the points you will make in the draft. Then write the draft using the worksheet as a guide. You can also create an outline worksheet as a computer file.

❋ WRITE AN INFORMAL OUTLINE

An informal outline lists and groups your most important ideas. Typically, an informal outline includes

- Your thesis idea.
- Your major points to support the thesis.
- Some of the ideas that support your major points.

Here is an example of an informal outline for an essay arguing that public school students should not have to wear uniforms.

Thesis idea

Public school students should not have to wear uniforms.

Introduction

Mention the problems public schools face (attendance, violence, low test scores, demoralized teachers and students) and explain that uniforms are not the solution to these problems.

Body paragraphs

The Constitution does not allow public school students to be forced to wear uniforms.
—Some students will wear and some won't.
—Preferential treatment will result.
If everyone dresses the same, there will be no self-expression.
—Students need to express their individuality in a harmless way.
—Most other aspects of education require conformity.
Deal with argument that uniforms save money and eliminate "clothing competition."
—The savings aren't worth the problems uniforms cause.
—People need to learn how to handle competition.

Conclusion

The problems in our schools must be solved, but uniforms won't do it.

FIGURE 1

Outline Worksheet

Paragraph I

   1. Opening comments to stimulate interest: _____

   _____

   _____

   2. Thesis statement: _____

   _____

   _____

Paragraph II

   1. Main point (topic sentence idea): _____

   _____

   _____

   2. Supporting details to develop main point: _____

   _____

   _____

Paragraph III

   1. Main point (topic sentence idea): _____

   _____

   _____

   2. Supporting details to develop main point: _____

   _____

   _____

Note: Continue in this way until all main points are treated.

Final paragraph

Ideas to provide closure: _____

_____

_____

_____

✳ CONSTRUCT AN OUTLINE MAP

To develop the map, use your list of generated ideas to fill in a copy of the form shown in Figure 2 below.

FIGURE 2

Outline Map			
Thesis: _____			
Main Point (Topic Sentence Idea)	Main Point (Topic Sentence Idea)	Main Point (Topic Sentence Idea)	Main Point (Topic Sentence Idea)
Supporting Detail	Supporting Detail	Supporting Detail	Supporting Detail

Concluding points: _____
_____
_____
_____

To complete the map, write in your thesis and place one main point at the top of each column. (For two main points, you will have two columns; three main points will mean three columns, and so on.) In the columns under each main point, write the supporting ideas that will develop the main point. Then note what your concluding point(s) will be.

Before you begin drafting, determine the relevance of ideas by checking what is in each column against the main point at the top, and you can check the relevance of each main point by comparing it to the thesis. Write your draft from the map by allowing each column to be a body paragraph, with each main point expressed in a topic sentence.

WRITE AN ABSTRACT

An **abstract** is a brief summary. Before you draft, write a one-paragraph abstract of what you plan to say in your writing. Include only the main points, and leave out the details that will expand on those points. Then read over your abstract to check that the main points follow logically one to the next. If they do not, try another abstract, placing your ideas in a different order. When you draft, you can flesh out the abstract into a full-length piece of writing.

Part II

A Troubleshooting Guide to Drafting

Drafting, which is your first attempt to write down your ideas, results in a **first draft**. Most people write very rough first drafts, so don't be discouraged if your first draft is ragged. No matter how rough it is, your draft can be reworked until it is reader ready.

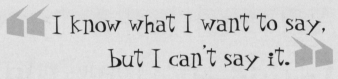 **I know what I want to say,
but I can't say it.**

Have you tried these?

❏ Writing a letter **(p. 44)** ❏ Walking away **(p. 45)**

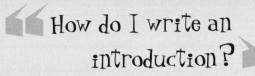 **How do I write an
introduction?**

Have you tried these?

❏ Providing background **(p. 48)** ❏ Using a quotation **(p. 49)**

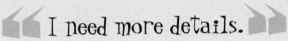 **I need more details.**

Have you tried these?

❏ Using your experience **(p. 53)** ❏ Giving examples **(p. 55)**

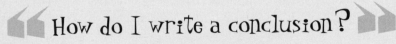 **How do I write a conclusion?**

Have you tried these?

❏ Providing a summary **(p. 61)** ❏ Asking a question **(p. 62)**

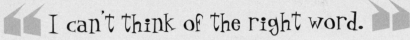 **I can't think of the right word.**

Have you tried these?

❏ Using a natural style **(p. 64)** ❏ Freewriting **(p. 65)**

CHAPTER FOUR

"I Know What I Want to Say, but I Can't Say It."

Y ou think you know what you want to say, so you settle in at your desk with a big bag of Doritos. Then disaster strikes: You know what you want to say, but the words don't come out right—or they don't come out at all. If this happens to you, know that you are not alone. Plenty of writers experience the same block. To get past the block, use the techniques described in this chapter.

THINK POSITIVELY

If you think negatively, writer's block can worsen, so replace negative thoughts with positive thoughts. For example, rather than think, "I'll never figure this out," tell yourself, "I just need a little more time, and I will know what to write." Instead of, "This is too hard," think, "I will master this challenge." Positive thoughts motivate; negative thoughts paralyze.

ELIMINATE DISTRACTIONS

Are you trying to write with the TV playing in the background? With your room-mate rummaging around looking for a missing left sneaker? With the street department outside tearing up the pavement with a jackhammer? Few people can write when distractions disrupt their focus, so getting past writer's block may be as simple as finding a place to write that is free of distractions.

SET INTERMEDIATE GOALS

At the beginning of a writing project, the finish line can seem so far away that you feel stressed. This stress can lead to writer's block. Try breaking the task down into manageable steps. For example, the first time you sit down, aim to come up with five ideas and a scratch outline. The second time, just draft the introduction. The third time, draft two more paragraphs. If you work toward the completion of intermediate goals, the project will be less daunting.

✳ ALLOW YOUR DRAFT TO BE ROUGH

If you find yourself starting a draft, hitting the delete key or crumpling up the paper and pitching it to the floor, starting another draft, hitting the delete key or crumpling up the paper and pitching it to the floor, over and over again, you may be expecting too much too soon. Remember, a first draft is *supposed* to be rough. Instead of starting over, force yourself to go from start to finish in one sitting to get raw material to shape during revision.

✳ WRITE IN A NEW PLACE

A change of scenery can help you break through a block by giving you a fresh perspective. If you usually write in one place, try another. Go to the library, the park, or a local diner. If you write in your room, try the lounge or a classroom or the dining hall.

✳ SWITCH YOUR WRITING TOOLS

If you write with a pen, try a pencil or a computer. If you use a computer, try a pen. If you like lined paper, try unlined. If you like legal pads, try stationery. Do anything to make the writing *feel* different.

✳ WRITE ON A DAILY SCHEDULE

Professional writers are disciplined about their work. They make themselves sit down at the same time each day to write for a specific number of hours. Follow the lead of the professionals and push past the block by forcing yourself to write at a certain time each day for a specific length of time.

✳ WRITE A LETTER TO A FRIEND

If you think of the reader at the other end judging your work, you may freeze. Try writing your draft as if it were a letter to a friend who cares about you and who will value you regardless of how well you write. When your audience is shifted to a person you feel comfortable with, you can relax and allow the words to emerge. After writing a draft this way, revise to make your work suitable for your intended reader and to shape it into an essay.

✳ WRITE FOR YOURSELF

Forget your reader and write the draft in a way that pleases *you*. Later when you polish your work, you can make the changes necessary for your real audience.

✳ USE A NATURAL STYLE

If you try too hard to achieve what you think is a "college" style, you may create a block. To solve this problem, write as you normally speak, and the words should flow more easily. After drafting this way, revise if the writing is too conversational or informal.

Unnatural   The garrulous male juvenile, who upon cursory examination gave the appearance of being about 12, nettled the orator.

More natural   The talkative boy, who looked about 12, annoyed the speaker.

✳ SPEAK INTO A RECORDER

You may have trouble writing but not talking. Try speaking your draft into a recorder. Afterward, you can transcribe the audio to get your draft.

✳ REREAD OFTEN

If you get blocked in the middle, go back and reread your draft from the beginning. Doing so can give you momentum to propel you past the block. Rereading can be a reminder of your thesis, purpose, and organizational strategy, a reminder that keeps you on track.

✳ WALK AWAY

When the words won't come, you may need time away to relax and let things simmer. Take a walk, listen to music, play tennis, take a shower, make a sandwich, read a magazine, clean a drawer, or pot a plant. Time away can provide an incubation period, so when you start to write again you are no longer stuck.

✳ CONCENTRATE ON WHAT YOU CAN DO AND SKIP WHAT YOU CAN'T DO

Begin with whatever point you feel confident writing, and go from there. For example, if you're stuck on the introduction, write the rest of your essay and then go back to the beginning. (If you write your introduction last, write a thesis on scratch paper to focus your writing.) If you start out just fine, but begin to struggle along the way, you may be dwelling on the trouble spots and losing momentum. To solve this problem, skip the trouble spots: If you can't think of the right word, leave a blank and add it later; if you sense some detail is not working, underline it for later consideration and press on.

✳ RESIST THE TEMPTATION TO REWRITE AS YOU DRAFT

If you constantly rewrite what you have already written, you can get stuck in one place—maybe polishing the introduction over and over, or tinkering endlessly with the detail to support your first point. Although some writers do well if they revise as they go, others get bogged down. If you get bogged down, push forward even if what you have already written is in sorry shape. You can revise later.

✳ WRITE FAST AND DON'T LOOK BACK

If you write fast, you will have no time to worry about how well you are saying things. You will only be able to get things down the best way you can at the moment. Later when you revise, you can rework things as needed.

✳ WRITE THE TITLE

Sometimes a terrific title will push you forward through a block because it suggests an approach or an organization or an introduction.

✳ STOP BEFORE YOU BLOCK

To prevent a block, take a break while your ideas are still flowing. Just be sure to leave yourself a note about what to write next, so when you return you can pick up the thread and keep moving forward.

✳ WRITE AN OUTLINE

If you have generated good ideas and you still have trouble drafting, you may be unsure what ideas you should write first, second, third, and so on. An outline can help. (For information on outlining, consult Chapter 3.)

✳ RETURN TO IDEA GENERATION

You may *not* have a clear enough idea of what you want to say, so you may need to return to idea generation. Try a favorite technique to clarify your thinking or to flesh out some existing ideas. Or try a technique you have not used before. (See Chapter 1 for suggestions.)

✳ USE YOUR ESSAY FORMAT

If you draft at the computer, use the same margins, spacing, and font that you will use for your final essay. (If your instructor has specified a particular format, be sure to use that one.) Because your draft will more closely resemble your finished essay, you may get a more realistic sense of length and development.

✳ SPLIT YOUR COMPUTER SCREEN

On one part of the screen, display your tentative thesis, outline, or idea generation material; on the other part, display your draft. This way, you can easily refer to your prewriting material as you write.

✳ WRITE INVISIBLE NOTES

Many word processing programs allow you to write notes that appear on your screen but not on the printed page. If you want to record an idea or make a comment for later consideration, and you do not want to interrupt your drafting, use this capability to write on your draft. The comments will not appear on your paper copy, but they will be saved for you to view later.

✳ CUT AND PASTE

If you generate ideas on the computer, you can cut and paste some or all of that material into a first draft. Of course, you will need to revise that material later, but it can work well as a departure point.

CHAPTER FIVE

"I'm Having Trouble with My Introduction."

The first day of school, the first day on a new job, a first date—starting out can be hard. Starting a piece of writing can also be difficult, even if you have generated plenty of ideas. However, the strategies in this chapter can help. In the sample introductions below, the thesis statements are underlined as a study aid. Be sure to notice that the thesis can come at the beginning, middle, or end of the introduction.

EXPLAIN WHY YOUR TOPIC IS IMPORTANT

Let your readers know why your topic is important, and you can engage their interest. Say your essay will explain to residents of your town how they can eliminate cigarette advertising on billboards. Your introduction can explain why residents should want to eliminate this advertising in the first place, like this:

> Other than the tobacco companies and a few nicotine addicts who live in denial, few people dispute the fact that cigarettes are a serious—even a deadly—health hazard. Because cigarettes are so dangerous, laws prohibit their advertising on television. Unfortunately, a similar ban does not exist for all print media. As a result, many people are enticed to begin smoking after viewing the ads that promise everything from "pure smoking pleasure" to fun, friends, and romance. <u>Thus, we should lobby local officials to ban cigarette advertising on billboards in our town.</u>

PROVIDE BACKGROUND INFORMATION

What should your reader know to appreciate or understand your topic? What information would establish a context for your essay? The answers to these questions can provide background information in the introduction. For example, assume you will argue that more federal money should be spent to educate children about the dangers of tobacco. Your introduction could supply background information about past efforts in this area, like this:

> In the 1990s President Clinton began an initiative to reduce tobacco use by children. In 1995, the FDA attempted to reduce the appeal of cigarette advertising to young people by limiting ads to black and white, text-only and by prohibiting cigarette ads on billboards near schools. Nonetheless, the effects have been insufficient, and the public health crisis continues as children start smoking at younger ages. <u>Clearly, the federal government must devote considerably more money and resources to educating children about tobacco.</u>

Tell a Story

Tell a story that is related to your topic or that illustrates your thesis. For example, if your essay shows that modern conveniences can be more trouble than they are worth, the following introduction with a story could be effective:

> The morning of my job interview, I woke up an hour earlier than usual and took special pains with my hair and makeup. I ate a light, sensible breakfast, which managed to hit bottom despite the menagerie of winged insects fluttering around my stomach. I drove the parkway downtown, nervously biting my lower lip the whole way. I had to park three long blocks from the office building where the interview was to take place, and by the time I got to the building I was completely windblown. Breathless, I gasped my name to the receptionist, who explained that my interview would have to be postponed. The personnel director had never made it in. It seems her electricity was off, and she could not get her car out of the garage because the door was controlled by an electric opener. That's when I knew for sure that <u>modern conveniences can be downright inconvenient</u>.

Use an Interesting Quotation

If someone has said something applicable to your thesis and said it particularly well, you can engage interest by quoting the remark. Just be sure that the quotation is interesting and not an overused expression like "better safe than sorry" or "the early bird gets the worm." Here is an example:

> Everyone seems to agree that we learn from our mistakes and that failure can be more instructive than success. Why, then, are students denied the opportunity to repeat courses without penalty? <u>So that we can profit from our mistakes, the administration should allow students to take courses three times and record the highest grade on our transcripts.</u> After all, as General Colin Powell has said, "There are no secrets to success. It is the result of preparation, hard work, and learning from failure."

PROVIDE RELEVANT STATISTICS

Relevant statistics, particularly if they are surprising, can engage a reader.

> According to our campus newspaper, this college has spent $25 million for campus renovations in the past five years. During the same period, enrollment has dropped by 2,273 students, and 112 fewer people are employed here. These figures suggest that the administration cares more about buildings than people. <u>It is time to reverse the trend and work to increase enrollment, faculty, and staff.</u>

PLAGIARISM ALERT

When you quote someone or use a statistic—whether you do so in your introduction or elsewhere in your essay—you must indicate the source. Notice that in the sample introductions above, the source of the quotation is given with the words "as General Colin Powell has said," and the source of the statistic is given with the words "According to our campus newspaper."

FIND COMMON GROUND WITH YOUR READER

Identify a point of view or experience you and your reader share. Presenting this common ground in an introduction can create a bond between you and your reader. In the following introduction, the common ground is a shared school experience:

> <u>If we abolish compulsory attendance, everyone will be better off.</u> Think back to when you were in high school. Remember the kids who caused all the trouble, the ones who disrupted the teacher and made it difficult for the rest of the class to learn? They were the students who did not want to be in school anyway and made things miserable for the students who did want to be there. Now imagine how much more learning would have occurred if the troublemakers had been allowed to quit school and get jobs.

DESCRIBE SOMETHING

Description adds interest and liveliness to writing.

> At 5 feet 3 inches and 170 pounds, Mr. Daria looked like a meatball. His stringy black hair, always in need of a cut, kept sliding into his eyes, and his too-tight shirts would not stay tucked into his too-tight polyester pants. He wore

the same sport coat every day; it was easily identified by the grease splotch on the left lapel. <u>Yes, Mr. Daria was considered a nerd by most of the student body, but to me he was the best history teacher on the planet.</u>

✳ ASK ONE OR MORE QUESTIONS RELATED TO YOUR THESIS

You can arouse curiosity and ease your reader into your topic if you ask one or more questions related to your thesis, like this:

Why don't people do the right thing anymore? Why are so many business-people and politicians making the news because they fail to act ethically? Perhaps the answer is that people no longer know what ethical behavior is—they need to be taught. <u>For that reason, ethics classes should become a regular part of the public school curriculum.</u>

✳ BEGIN WITH THE THESIS AND THE POINTS YOU WILL DISCUSS

Sometimes the direct approach is the best. You can begin by stating your thesis and the main points you will discuss, like this:

<u>Carolyn Hotimsky is the best candidate for mayor for two reasons.</u> First, as president of the city council, she demonstrated leadership ability. Second, as chief investment counselor for First City Bank, she learned about sound fiscal management.

✳ KEEP IT SHORT

If you are having trouble with something, why make it as long as possible? If your introduction is proving troublesome, just write your thesis and one or two other sentences, and get on with the rest of your writing. If all else fails, just write your thesis and go on to your first point to be developed.

✳ WRITE IT LAST

If you cannot come up with an introduction, write the rest of your piece and then return to the introduction. With the rest of your writing drafted, an approach may come to mind. However, if you skip your introduction, jot down a working thesis on scratch paper and check it periodically to be sure you do not stray into unrelated areas.

Turn Your Conclusion into Your Introduction

Your last paragraph may work better as an introduction than as a conclusion. To find out, move your conclusion to the beginning of your writing. With some fine-tuning, you may be able to turn the conclusion into a strong introduction. Of course, you will have to write a new conclusion, but that may prove easier than wrestling with the introduction.

CHAPTER SIX

"How Do I Back Up What I Say?"

NO doubt, you are a wonderful human being who would never lie. Nevertheless, no experienced reader will believe you unless you support your statements with proof and explanation. The strategies in this chapter can help you back up what you say.

USE YOUR OWN EXPERIENCE

Your own life experiences can provide convincing evidence. Say, for example, that you are discussing problems created by computers, and you make the point that computers often contribute to procrastination. You might write a paragraph like the following, based on your own experience:

> Computers can be great time wasters. The last time I sat down to write a paper, I found myself playing "Words with Friends" instead of drafting. The next thing I knew, an hour had gone by. I got myself back on task, but when I became stuck, I decided to check my e-mail. By the time I read and responded to five messages, another 20 minutes was lost. I tried to work on my paper again, but I was lured away by Facebook. I couldn't believe it when the clock in the corner of my screen showed that I had spent an hour posting on walls and chatting on Skype. When I realized how much time I had wasted, I went straight back to my paper, but I was so tired that I know I didn't give it my best efforts. I probably would have done better had I used a pen and paper.

Be aware that in some disciplines and for some audiences and purposes, personal experience may not qualify as convincing support. For example, in a research paper about computers and procrastination for a psychology class, your own experience with procrastination will not be convincing because it can be seen as an isolated case. However, a study reporting that one-third of all college students play computer games instead of studying can serve as convincing evidence.

USE YOUR OBSERVATIONS

Your observations of the world can offer excellent support for ideas. Say you are discussing the trend to require volunteerism in high schools. Your observation of the volunteer work students do at local high schools could lead to this paragraph:

> Students can learn a great deal when they are required to perform volunteer service. However, care must be taken with the kinds of activities they are allowed to engage in. At our local high school, students were at first involved in such worthy activities as volunteering in hospitals, purchasing groceries for elderly neighbors, and coaching youth soccer. Now they receive volunteer credit for such dubious activities as helping out in the school office during study hall, working on theater sets for the senior play, and selling programs at football games. I doubt very much is learned from such work.

TALK TO OTHERS

If a statement in your draft needs more backup, ask people you trust for ideas. You can even e-mail the section to a reliable reader and ask for suggestions.

TELL A STORY

Search your own experience for brief stories that can drive home your points. Consider this passage:

> Distance running is an excellent sport for adolescents because even if they do not finish near the front of the pack, they can still feel good about themselves. Shaving a few seconds off an earlier time or completing a difficult course can be a genuine source of pride for a young runner.

Now notice how the addition of a brief story helps prove the point:

> Distance running is an excellent sport for adolescents because even if they do not finish near the front of the pack, they can still feel good about themselves. Shaving a few seconds off an earlier time or completing a difficult course can be a genuine source of pride for a young runner. I remember a race I ran as a sophomore. I was recovering from a miserable cold and not in peak condition. Just after completing the first mile, I developed a cramp in my side. However, I was determined to finish, no matter how long it took me. Quarter mile by quarter mile, I ran rather haltingly. My chest was tight from lack of training because I had been sick, and my side hurt, but still I kept on. Eventually, I crossed the finish line, well back in the standings. However, I could not have been more proud of myself if I had won. I showed that I had what it took to finish, even though the going was tough.

✳ DESCRIBE PEOPLE AND PLACES

Description creates vivid images that help readers to see and hear the way you see and hear. It also adds interest and vitality to writing. Consider this passage:

> The best teacher I ever had was Mrs. Suarez, who taught me algebra in the ninth grade. But even more than teaching me algebra, Mrs. Suarez showed me compassion during a very difficult time in my life. I will always be grateful for her understanding and encouragement when I needed them most.
>
> In the ninth grade, I was a troubled teen, a victim of a difficult home life. Somehow Mrs. Suarez recognized my pain and approached me one day. . . .

Now notice the interest created with the addition of description:

> The best teacher I ever had was Mrs. Suarez, who taught me algebra in the ninth grade. But even more than teaching me algebra, Mrs. Suarez showed me compassion during a very difficult time in my life. To look at this woman, a person would never guess what a caring nature she had. With wire stiff hair teased and lacquered into a bouffant, Mrs. Suarez looked like a hard woman. Her face, heavily wrinkled, had a scary, witchlike quality that fit the shrill voice she used to reprimand 14-year-old sinners who neglected their homework. She always stood ramrod straight with her 120 pounds evenly distributed over her orthopedic shoes. Many a student has been frightened by a first look at this no-nonsense woman. However, appearances are, indeed, deceptive, for Mrs. Suarez was not the witch she looked to be. In fact, I will always be grateful for her understanding and encouragement when I needed them most.

✳ GIVE EXAMPLES

Nothing clarifies or proves a point like a well-chosen example. Examples can come from personal experience, observation, reading, research, or classroom experience. Assume you have stated that television commercials cause us to buy products we do not need. You could back up that point with examples you have observed, like this:

> Television commercials often make people want products they do not need. For example, Tony the Tiger urges children to eat highly sugared cereal, and gorgeous, bikini-clad women romp on the beach, luring men to consume beer. Before Christmas, expensive toys based on the latest action hero are advertised relentlessly, until children are convinced they cannot survive without them. Of course, the worst offenders are the advertisers of hair color, mascara, lipstick, perfume, and teeth whiteners, who convince women they cannot be attractive without a drawer full of these products.

You could also take an example from personal experience (the time you went to a tax preparer because a commercial wrongly convinced you that you could not do your own taxes); you could draw an example from research (talk to others about unnecessary products they have purchased as a result of commercials); or you could cite an example you learned in the classroom (perhaps statistics on the number of people who buy a particular unnecessary product).

GIVE REASONS

Reasons help prove that something is true. Let's say your point is that final examinations should be eliminated. These reasons could help prove your point: Finals create too much anxiety; they do not really show what a student knows; placing considerable emphasis on one examination is not fair; and some students test poorly. Here is how those reasons might appear in a paragraph:

> Final examinations should be eliminated because they are not a sound educational practice. These exams create too much anxiety among students. Students worry so much about their performance that they lose sleep, stop eating, and show other signs of stress. Certainly, they cannot demonstrate what they know under such circumstances. They also cannot show what they really know because the exams cannot test everything—just what the teacher wants to test. As a result, some of what a student knows may never be asked for. Furthermore, if the test is poorly constructed (and many of them are), students may further be kept from demonstrating their real learning. Finally, many students are poor test takers. They know the material, but they cannot demonstrate their knowledge because they have never mastered the art of taking tests.

SHOW SIMILARITIES OR DIFFERENCES

Assume you are writing about ways to improve the quality of life in nursing homes, and you make the point that nursing homes should allow residents to have pets. The following paragraph shows how you can back up your point by citing similarities:

> Because nursing homes have long recognized the value of having young children visit residents, preschool classes are often invited to spend time in the facilities. Allowing the residents to have pets would be similarly beneficial. Just as the children do, the pets would provide companionship for the residents and give them an opportunity to express affection. Also, just as it does with children, the interaction with pets would provide intellectual stimulation and an opportunity to forget about infirmities. Of course, in one respect, pets are better than children: They do not have to go home at the end of the day because they already are home and can continue to make life better for residents.

Now assume you want to argue that having pets in nursing homes is not a good idea. Showing differences can help you back up your point.

> Some people claim that having pets in nursing homes would be beneficial in the same way that having preschoolers visit there is beneficial. This contention is not true. First, children do not add cost to a nursing home or its residents. Their parents feed them and take care of medical expenses, but the residents or nursing home would have to assume these expenses for pets. Also, because children are supervised by their teachers, residents need not watch them very closely. Pets, on the other hand, need to be restrained from entering the rooms

of residents who do not want to be near them. Since many residents cannot supervise the animals all the time, an already overburdened staff would have even more responsibility. Finally, children go home at the end of the day, but pets stay and require ongoing care, which can drain nursing home resources.

✳ EXPLAIN CAUSES OR EFFECTS

If you are writing about sex education in schools and make the point that it should be mandatory, you can back up this point by citing the positive effects of sex education, like this:

> Sex education's most obvious benefit is increased knowledge. Since it is unlikely that sexually active teens will start to abstain, increased knowledge about birth control will prevent unwanted pregnancy. Furthermore, the same knowledge can help teens protect themselves against sexually transmitted disease. When fewer teens become pregnant, more of them will stay in school and not fall victim to unemployment, drugs, and crime. When more teens protect themselves against sexually transmitted diseases, fewer will die.

If you want to emphasize the need for sex education by citing the pressure on teenagers to become sexually active, you might explain what causes teenagers to become sexually active, like this:

> One reason teenagers are sexually active at a younger age is that they are bombarded by sexual messages. On MTV and YouTube, videos are populated with women wearing next to nothing; men and women are touching, groping, and grinding in sexually provocative ways. Rock lyrics glorify teen sex as healthy rebellion and a sign of independence. Movies, too, send sexual messages. Sex scenes and nudity are frequent in PG-13 movies and are standard fare in R-rated movies that teens have easy access to.

To discover causes, ask yourself, "Why does this happen?" To discover effects, ask yourself, "After this happens, then what?" For example, ask, "Why do teenagers engage in sex?" and you might get the answer, "To be more like an adult." The desire to be mature then becomes a cause. Ask yourself, "After sex education courses are offered, then what?" If you get the answer, "Teenagers learn safe sex practices," you have an effect of sex education.

✳ EXPLAIN HOW SOMETHING IS MADE OR DONE

Assume you are discussing simple things people can do to combat prejudice. If you make the point that people do not have to put up with racial, ethnic, or sexist humor, you might back up that point by explaining how a person can deal with such offensive humor, like this:

> Many people do not know how to respond when they are told a racial, ethnic, or sexist joke, so they laugh politely, even though they feel uncomfortable. A

better approach is to say something simple, such as, "I don't find such jokes funny." Then you can turn the conversation to a neutral topic. If the joke was told to several people, and you do not want to embarrass the speaker, draw him or her aside later and say, "I'm sure you did not mean to, but you made me very uncomfortable when you told your joke." Both of these approaches let the speaker know that hurtful jokes are not universally welcome.

✳ EXPLAIN WHAT WOULD HAPPEN IF YOUR ASSERTION WERE NOT ADOPTED

Assume that you are advocating the passage of a tax levy to fund the building of a new high school. To help make your point, you can explain what would happen if the levy did not pass, like this:

> Without the passage of the levy, funds will not be available to finance a new high school. Without the high school, our children will suffer. The current building is too small, and enrollment is projected to increase over the next five years. Thus, classes will be overcrowded. Furthermore, the current building lacks an auditorium, making it impossible to have a theater program. The lack of an auditorium also means assemblies and band concerts must be held in the gym, where the acoustics are poor and the seats are uncomfortable. Most worrisome is the fact that the renovations required in the existing building, including asbestos removal, a new roof, and an updated heating system, will cost almost as much as a new school. If we spend money on these renovations, the children will reap no benefits, the way they would with a new building.

✳ CONSIDER OPPOSING VIEWS

Think about the opinions of those who disagree with you. You can acknowledge a compelling point and offer your counterargument. For example, if you were advocating warning labels on CDs and music downloads with sexually explicit lyrics, you could write the following:

> People against warning labels cite the "forbidden fruit" argument. They say that young people will be encouraged to buy music with the labels, expressly because they are being warned away from them. To some extent this is true. However, the labels will still provide a guideline for parents who want to buy music for their children. They will also create an atmosphere of acceptability. Although young people may ignore them, the labels still send a message that some things are more appropriate than others for teenagers. This atmosphere is an improvement over the current "anything goes" climate that sends the message that teens can buy and do whatever they please.

Use Material from Outside Sources

Statistics, facts, quotations, and ideas from outside sources can provide important support for many topics. These sources can include your textbooks and class lectures, newspapers, magazines, and sources you discover in the library or on the Internet. You should judge the credibility of any material from outside sources according to the guidelines on page 157.

PLAGIARISM ALERT

When you use material from an outside source—whether that source is electronic or paper—document that material according to the guidelines explained in Chapter 29. However, if the material is common knowledge or a matter of public record, you do not need to document it. For example, you do not need to document the fact that Sacramento is the capital of California because the fact is common knowledge or that Richard Nixon died in 1994 because the date is a matter of public record.

Use the Word Count Feature

Sometimes the number of words that develop an idea is a clue to how well developed the idea is. Most word processing programs will tally the number of words in a section you highlight. Although word count is not by itself a reliable indication of sufficient support, it does offer one measure for you to consider.

CHAPTER SEVEN

"I Don't Know How to End."

Imagine that you go to the movies to see the latest action film. The beginning is thrilling—you're on the edge of your seat; the middle is very exciting—you're completely caught up in the plot. Then the ending comes—and it's awful. When you walk out of the theater, you probably do not talk about how good the beginning and middle were. Instead, you probably complain about how bad the ending was. Why? Because endings form the last impression, the one that is most remembered.

Your conclusion forms your reader's final impression. If you write a weak conclusion, no matter how strong the rest of your essay is, your reader will feel let down. If you have trouble ending your writing, try the strategies in this chapter.

Explain the Significance of Your Thesis

Ideas in the conclusion are most likely to be remembered because of their placement at the end. Therefore, the conclusion can be a good place to state the significance of your thesis. For example, assume your thesis is that being cut from the junior high school basketball team had a lifelong impact on you. Your conclusion can state the significance of that thesis:

> Because being cut from the team shattered my self-esteem at a young age, I have struggled all my life with feelings of inadequacy. I have doubted my ability because the coach, whose judgment I trusted, told me that I wasn't good enough.

PROVIDE A HELPFUL SUMMARY

Summarizing your main points is a service to your reader if you have written a long essay or one with complex ideas. After reading a long or complicated writing, a reader will appreciate a review. However, if your essay is short or if the ideas are easily grasped, a summary is a boring rehash of previously covered material.

EXPLAIN THE CONSEQUENCES OF IGNORING YOUR THESIS

If you are writing to persuade your reader to think or act a certain way, you can close by explaining what would happen if your reader did not follow your recommendation. Assume, for example, that you are writing to convince your reader that a drug education program should be instituted in the local elementary school. After giving your reasons, you could close like this:

> If we do not have a drug education program in the earliest grades, we miss the opportunity to influence our children when they are the most impressionable. If we miss this opportunity to influence them when they are young and responsive to adult pressure, we run the risk of losing our children to powerful peer pressure to experiment with drugs.

CONCLUDE WITH A POINT YOU WANT TO EMPHASIZE

Anything placed at the end is emphasized. Therefore, you can conclude with your most important point, the one you want underscored in your reader's mind. For example, if you are explaining the differences between child-rearing practices of today and those of 60 years ago, you could end like this:

> The most telling difference between child-rearing practices of today and those of 60 years ago is that today's parents are less rigid. Unlike the parents of 60 years ago, they are less concerned with doing everything on schedule and by the book. Babies are not forced to eat and sleep at specific times but may do so when they are hungry and sleepy. Today's parents trust their instincts more than they trust the child care books used by parents of the past. Thus, they are more likely to do what they think is right and not worry about what the "authorities" say.

RESTATE YOUR THESIS FOR EMPHASIS

If you decide to close by restating your thesis, be sure the restatement is effective emphasis rather than boring repetition. Also, avoid restating in the same language you used previously. Restate the thesis a *new* way.

✳ SUGGEST A COURSE OF ACTION

State a remedy to a problem your essay discusses, or call your reader to action. For example, if your essay explains the reason for declining enrollment at your school, you can suggest a course of action in the conclusion:

> The reasons for our declining enrollment are complex, but the solution to the problem is clear. First, we should hire a recruitment specialist to seek new students. At the same time, we should begin a marketing campaign, complete with local television and radio spots, to attract area people, so they attend school here rather than out of state. Finally, we should hire a marketing firm to discover what potential students are seeking and try to meet those desires. Yes, these measures are expensive, but the money will be well spent if we can return enrollment figures to their previous high levels.

✳ ASK A QUESTION

You can leave your reader thinking about your thesis if you close with a suitable question, as exemplified in this conclusion for an essay arguing against raising the speed limit on state routes:

> If the speed limit is raised, truckers will save money, as will those who ship their goods on trucks. And while studies do not show that the higher speed limit will mean more accidents, they suggest that the accidents that do occur will involve more fatalities. Do we really want to save money but lose lives?

✳ LOOK TO THE FUTURE

Sometimes you can look ahead to the time beyond your essay. Say your essay explains the benefits and drawbacks of purchasing goods on the Internet. You could close by looking to the future, like this:

> Although e-commerce has become increasingly popular, the next five years will show a marked decline as people return to brick-and-mortar stores. The novelty of online shopping will wear off as consumers admit to the difficulties of shopping for clothing and gifts they cannot touch, try on, or examine firsthand. Increased shipping costs will render online shopping too expensive, and fears about electronic security breaches will deter many consumers. Finally, consumers often miss the social and recreational aspects of shopping and will return to traditional stores for the simple human interaction they offer.

✳ COMBINE APPROACHES

You can combine any two or more approaches to create a strong conclusion. For example, you can summarize main points and then make a recommendation, or you can restate your thesis and then ask a question.

Echo Your Introduction

Create an "echo" by repeating a phrase, image, or idea from your introduction, but put a spin on it. For example, read the introduction on page 50 that illustrates providing a relevant statistic. You could echo that introduction with the conclusion that follows. The echo is underlined and the spin is double underlined as a study aid:

> No institution that <u>cares more about buildings than people</u> can survive, let alone thrive. <u>Our administration must step up its recruiting efforts to enroll more students, thereby creating the need for additional faculty and staff. If more buildings are needed as enrollment increases, then—and only then—should they be built.</u>

Keep It Short

If you have trouble with your conclusion, keep it short. Although you do not want to end abruptly, do not take something that is a problem and stretch it out longer than necessary. A perfectly effective conclusion can be only one or two sentences.

Chapter Eight

"I Can't Think of the Right Word."

You're writing along, and just as your confidence begins to surge—wham! You're stuck because you can't think of the right word. You try all the usual techniques—chewing on the end of your pencil to squeeze the word into the tip, rubbing your forehead to massage the word into your brain, and glaring at the computer screen to will the word to appear—but nothing helps. The next time the word you need escapes you, try the techniques in this chapter.

Write in a Natural Style

You may be straining for an overly "sophisticated" style, a style you think will impress your reader. As a result, words escape you because you are seeking ones that were never a natural part of your vocabulary in the first place. Return to a more natural style, and words should come more easily.

Unnatural   Attempting to ruminate her morning nourishment while simultaneously communicating the events that transpired, Emma began to choke on her victuals.

More natural Trying to tell what happened at the same time she was eating breakfast, Emma began to choke.

Skip the Problem and Return to It Later

If after a minute you cannot think of the right word, leave a blank space and push on. You can return to consider the problem again when you revise. When you return, the word may surface, and the problem will be solved. If not, you can try the other strategies in this chapter.

Use ITTS

ITTS stands for "*I'm trying to say.*" When you cannot find the right word, stop for a moment and say to yourself, "I'm trying to say ____." Imagine yourself explaining what you mean to a friend, and fill in the blank with the word or words you would speak to that friend. Then write the word or words in your draft. You may need several words or even a sentence to fill in the blank when originally you were seeking only a single word. That's fine.

Substitute a Phrase or a Sentence for a Troublesome Word

If you cannot take one path, take an alternate route: If you cannot think of the right word, try using a phrase or a whole sentence to express your idea instead.

Ask Around

If you cannot think of the word that is on the tip of your tongue, ask around. To anyone who will listen, just say, "Hey, what's the word for ____?" Writers are always glad to help each other.

Freewrite for Three Minutes

You may not be able to think of the right word because you are not certain about what you want to say. To clarify your thinking, try three minutes of freewriting, focusing on the idea you want the word to convey. (Freewriting is explained on page 21.) After the freewriting, try again to come up with the word.

Use Simple, Specific Words

Some people have trouble finding the right words because they think good writing uses words like *bumptious, egregious, panacea, parsimonious,* and *pusillanimous.* The truth is that good writing is clear, simple, and specific. You do not need the high-flown $50 words. Instead of *parsimonious,* use *stingy.*

Use the Thesaurus and Dictionary Wisely

The thesaurus and dictionary are excellent tools for finding the right word. Online, you can use the dictionary and thesaurus at Dictionary.com. However, be sure you understand the connotation (secondary meaning) of any word you draw from these sources. For example, *skinny* and *lean* may mean the same thing on one level, but because of their connotations, a person would rather be called *lean* than *skinny*. If you do not understand the connotations of a word, you can misuse it.

WRITE—THEN REWRITE—CLICHÉS

Cliché's are overworked expressions like "cold as ice," "free as a bird," "sadder but wiser," and "a chain is only as strong as its weakest link." Writers are usually cautioned to avoid clichés because they are boring. However, when you have trouble finding the right words, go ahead and use a cliché if it helps you capture an idea. You can rewrite it later when you revise.

Draft sentence with cliché   Fred and I never see *eye to eye*.

Revision   Fred and I disagree about everything from where to eat to whom to vote for.

WRITE—THEN REWRITE—SLANG

Slang expressions do not belong in formal writing. However, if you cannot think of the right words, you can use slang in your draft to capture your thought. When you revise, however, rewrite to eliminate the slang.

Draft sentence with slang   Michael was *jerking me around*.

Revision   Michael was making the situation difficult for me.

BUILD YOUR VOCABULARY

The more words you know, the easier it is to find the "right" one. If you need to build your vocabulary, take these steps:

1. Read what you enjoy at least 15 minutes every day. Magazines, detective fiction, romance novels, online newspapers, blogs, or poetry—it doesn't matter what you read; just read!

2. When you hear or read an unfamiliar word, write it in a notebook, along with the sentence the word appeared in. Look up the words you recorded, and write the meanings that fit the sentences.

3. Study the words in your notebook regularly and make an effort to use those words in your speech and writing.

4. Learn word clusters by noting similar words around the word you are looking up. Thus, when you look up *mesmerize* (to hypnotize or fascinate), you can also learn *mesmerism* (hypnotism).

5. Work crossword puzzles. You'll have fun and learn words.

6. Learn a word a day. At www.wordsmith.org you can sign up to have a new word and its meaning e-mailed to you each day.

PART III

A Troubleshooting Guide to Revising

First drafts *always* have problems—that's why they are called **rough drafts.** However, even the most troubled first draft gives you material to shape and improve. When you decide what to change and when you make those changes, you are **revising.** To revise, consider content, organization, and expression of ideas. Do not worry about grammar, spelling, capitalization, or punctuation just yet.

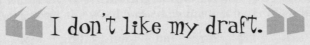
I don't like my draft.

Have you tried these?

❑ Walking away (p. 70)   ❑ Listening to the draft (p. 71)

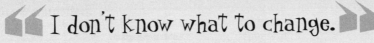
I don't know what to change.

Have you tried these?

❑ Thinking like a reader (p. 74)   ❑ Revising in stages (p. 76)

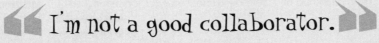
I'm not a good collaborator.

Have you tried these?

❑ Giving guidance (p. 79)   ❑ Evaluating responses (p. 81)

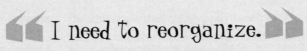
I need to reorganize.

Have you tried these?

❑ Using topic sentences (p. 83)   ❑ Repeating key words (p. 84)

My draft is the wrong length.

Have you tried these?

❑ Showing after telling (p. 87)   ❑ Checking your thesis (p. 90)

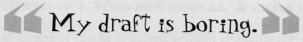

My draft is boring.

Have you tried these?

❑ Using specific words **(p. 93)**   ❑ Adding description **(p. 95)**

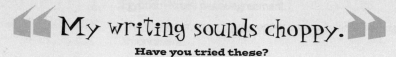

My writing sounds choppy.

Have you tried these?

❑ Varying sentence
openers **(p. 97)**   ❑ Combining sentences **(p. 99)**

"I Thought My Draft Was Better Than This."

You've just placed the final period at the end of the last sentence of your first draft, and you're feeling proud of yourself. So you lean back, put your feet up on the desk, and start to reread the masterpiece. However, as you read, your masterpiece doesn't seem nearly as good as you thought it was. Does this mean you have to start over? Probably not. Instead, try some of the suggestions in this chapter.

Be Realistic

Remember, a first draft is called a *rough* draft because your first attempt is supposed to have problems—even lots of them. Do not expect too much too soon. Instead, roll up your sleeves, get in there, and revise.

Walk Away

Before deciding about the quality of your draft, put it aside for a while to regain your objectivity. The longer you stay away, the better; but walk away for at least several hours—for a day if your deadline will allow. When you return to your draft and reread it, you may discover potential that you overlooked previously.

Share Your Draft

Are you being too hard on yourself? Instead of recognizing the potential in your draft, are you seeing only the rough spots? Share your draft with several people whose judgment you trust. Ask them what they like and what they want to read more about. Your readers' comments may reveal how much potential your draft has. (For more on reader response, see Chapter 11.)

Listen to Your Draft

Your draft may seem worse than it is if it is messy or written in sloppy handwriting or written in pencil or written on paper ripped out of a spiral notebook. In short, the appearance of the draft may affect your evaluation of it. To judge the worth of your draft more reliably, ask someone to read it to you. You may hear sections that are stronger than you realized.

Identify Two Changes That Will Improve Your Draft

Identify two changes that will make your draft better, and you may recognize how much potential your draft has. If you think it will help you accurately judge your draft, make those changes and *then* decide how you feel about your draft.

Write a Second Draft without Looking at the First

Writing a second draft without looking at the first can be successful because you often manage to retain the best parts of the first draft, eliminate the weakest parts, and add some new, effective material. The key is to avoid checking the first draft while writing the second.

Do Not Despair If You Must Start Over

Often we must discover what we do *not* want to do before we discover what we *do* want to do; we must learn what we *cannot* do before we learn what we *can* do. If you must begin again, do not be discouraged. Your first draft was not a waste of your time—it was groundwork that paved the way for your most recent effort.

Try to Salvage Something

If you begin again, try to salvage something. Perhaps you can use the same approach to your introduction or some of your examples or one main idea. Don't rip your draft to shreds or hit the delete key. Save your first draft in case you change your mind and want to use some of it later. If you compose at the computer, keep a "scraps" file for material you may decide to use at another time.

Do the Best You Can with What You Have

At some point you must force yourself to push forward, even if you are not completely comfortable with your draft. When time is running out, do the best you can with what you have and be satisfied that you have met your deadline.

Evaluate a Print Copy of Your Draft

If you compose at the computer, only part of a typed page is visible on your screen, making it hard to get a good overview of your writing. Thus, evaluating a print copy is important. If you draft with pen and paper, you may find it difficult to evaluate your draft objectively. Thus, you should type your draft and print out a copy to get a fresh perspective.

CHAPTER TEN

"I Don't Know What to Change."

Good news! You finished your first draft, and you are ready to dig in and make all those changes that will improve your writing. So you read your draft, but wait a minute—everything seems fine. *You* understand what you mean; everything seems clear and well developed to *you*. In fact, you can't figure out what changes to make and what all the revision fuss is about. The suggestions in this chapter can help.

WALK AWAY

Before revising, put your draft aside for a day, or longer if possible. The break can help you become more objective about your draft, so that when you return to revise, you can identify necessary changes.

CONSTRUCT A READER PROFILE

As the writer, you may have no trouble figuring out what you meant when you wrote all those words, but that does not guarantee that your reader will have an easy time of it. To revise successfully, view your draft as the reader and make changes to meet your reader's needs. Different readers will place different demands on a writer. For example, assume you are writing to convince your reader to vote for a school levy that will increase property taxes. If your audience is someone with children in the school system, explaining that the additional revenue will go toward enhancing the art and music curriculum may be sufficiently persuasive. However, if your reader is a childless retired person on a fixed income, this argument may not be very convincing. Instead, you may need to explain that better schools will cause the value of the reader's home to increase.

To evaluate your draft from your reader's perspective, construct a reader profile by answering the following 10 questions:

1. How much education does my reader have?

2. What are my reader's age, gender, race, nationality, and religion?

3. What are my reader's occupation and socioeconomic level?

4. What part of the country does my reader live in? Does my reader live in an urban or rural area?

5. What is my reader's political affiliation?

6. How familiar is my reader with my topic?

7. What does my reader need to know to appreciate my assertion?

8. How resistant will my reader be to my assertion?

9. How hard will I have to work to create interest in my topic?

10. Does my reader have any special interests or concerns that will affect reaction to my essay? Is my reader chiefly concerned with money? Career? The environment? Society? Religion? Family?

After answering these questions, review your draft with an eye toward providing detail suited to your reader's makeup. (Keep the reader profile questions as a computer file, and you can consult them each time you revise.)

❋ THINK LIKE YOUR READER

Asking the following questions as you study your draft can help you think like your reader and identify necessary changes:

1. Is there any place where my reader might lose interest?

2. Is there any place where my reader might not understand what I mean?

3. Is there any place where my reader is not likely to be convinced of the truth of my topic sentence or thesis?

❋ DESCRIBE YOUR DRAFT PARAGRAPH BY PARAGRAPH

Describing your draft paragraph by paragraph can help you analyze its strengths and weaknesses. To do this, summarize the content of paragraph 1; then explain how that paragraph meets your audience's needs and how it helps you achieve your purpose for writing. Next, summarize the content of paragraph 2; then explain how that paragraph meets your audience's needs and fulfills your purpose. Continue until you have described each paragraph. Read your description to identify points that stray from your thesis, ideas that need more development, and paragraphs that fail to meet your reader's needs or your writing purpose.

Type Your Draft

If you handwrote your draft, type it, print it out, and then read it over. Problems you overlook in your own handwriting are more apparent in type because the copy resembles printed material. As a result, it can be easier to be objective about the writing. Also, some mistakes may leap out at you. For example, a paragraph that ran a page in your handwritten copy may be fewer than four typed lines—a visual signal that more detail may be needed.

If you compose at the computer, you cannot get a good overview of your text on the screen, so be sure to study a print copy of your draft.

Listen to Your Draft

Read your draft out loud to hear problems that you overlook visually. Be sure to go slowly and read *exactly* what is on the page. If you read quickly, you may read what you *meant* to write rather than what you actually *did* write.

Some writers do well if they read their drafts into a recorder and play back the audio to listen for problems. Others prefer to have other people read their drafts to them. Another person's voice can help the writer pick up on problems.

Underline Main Points

Go through your draft and underline every main idea. Then check to see what appears after each underlined point. If one underlined point is immediately followed by another underlined point, you have not supported a main idea. Similarly, if an underlined idea is followed by only one or two sentences, you should consider whether you have enough support. If you compose at the computer, use the formatting features. Underline each main idea and then use boldface, highlighting, a new font, or a color to designate the support for each underlined idea. If very little appears in boldface, highlighting, or the different font or color, you likely need more supporting detail. For strategies for supporting points, see Chapter 6.

Highlight the Beginnings and Endings of Body Paragraphs

Using a highlighting pen on a paper draft or the highlighting feature on your computer, mark the first and last sentence or two of each body paragraph. Read only the highlighted material to assess whether your reader can follow the movement from main point to main point.

OUTLINE YOUR DRAFT AFTER WRITING IT

A good way to determine if your ideas follow logically one to the next is to outline your draft *after* writing it. If you have points that do not fit into the outline at the appropriate spots, you have discovered an organization problem.

REVISE IN STAGES

When you revise, you have a great deal to consider. To consider it all, revise in stages, using one of the following patterns.

Easy to Hard

Make the easy changes, and then make the more difficult changes. Take a break when you become tired or when you get stuck. Making the easy changes first helps you build momentum to carry you through the harder changes.

Hard to Easy

Make some of your more difficult changes, take a break, make some more of your difficult changes, take another break, and continue with the harder changes, taking breaks as needed. When you have finished the more difficult changes, tackle the easier ones. Some writers like the psychological lift that comes from getting the hard changes out of the way.

Paragraph by Paragraph

Revise your first paragraph until it is as strong as you can make it, and then go on to the next paragraph. Proceed paragraph by paragraph, taking a break after every paragraph or two.

Content–Organization–Effective Expression

First make all your content changes: adequate detail, relevant detail, specific detail, clarity, and suitable introduction and conclusion. Then take a break and check the organization: logical order of ideas, effective thesis, and clear topic sentences. Take another break and revise for sentence effectiveness: effective word choice, smooth flow, and helpful transitions.

SHARE YOUR INTRODUCTION AND CONCLUSION

To judge the effectiveness of your introduction and conclusion, type these parts separately, and give them to two or three people to read. Ask them whether they would be interested in reading something that opened and closed with these paragraphs.

✳Share Your Draft

Writers often ask reliable readers to react to their drafts and make suggestions. If you want to consider the opinions of readers, refer to the strategies in Chapter 11.

✳Pretend to Be Someone Else

To be more objective about your work, pretend you are someone else. Read your draft as the judge of a contest who will award you $10,000 for a prize-winning essay. Or become the editor of a magazine who is deciding what changes to make in the draft before publishing the piece. Or read as your worst enemy, someone who loves to find fault with your work.

✳Use a Revising Checklist

A revising checklist, like the following one, keeps you from overlooking some of the revision concerns. In addition, you can combine this checklist with reader response by asking a reliable reader to apply the checklist to your draft. You can also save it as a computer file to consult each time you revise. (The page numbers in parentheses refer to helpful pages in this book.)

Content

1. Does your writing have a clear thesis that accurately presents your focus? (page 31)
2. Does every point in your writing clearly relate to that thesis? (page 14)
3. Are all your generalizations, including your thesis, adequately supported? (pages 13–14)
4. Are all your points well suited to your audience and purpose? (pages 6 and 8)
5. Have you avoided stating the obvious? (page 95)
6. Does your introduction create interest in your topic? (page 48)
7. Does your conclusion provide a satisfying ending? (page 60)

Organization

1. Do your ideas follow logically one to the next? (pages 14–15)
2. Do your paragraphs follow logically one to the next? (pages 14–15)
3. Do the details in each paragraph relate to the topic sentence? (page 14)
4. Have you used transitions to show how ideas relate to each other? (page 84)

Expression

1. When you read your work aloud, does everything sound all right? (page 71)
2. Have you avoided wordiness? (page 91)

3. Have you eliminated clichés (overused expressions)? (page 94)

4. Have you used specific words? (page 93)

5. Did you use a variety of sentence openers? (page 97)

6. Have you used the active voice? (page 94)

7. Have you used action verbs rather than forms of *to be?* (page 94)

8. Have you used parallel structures? (page 99)

TRUST YOUR INSTINCTS

When your instincts tell you that something is wrong, assume you have a problem. Even if you cannot give the problem a name, you have identified something that needs to be reworked. Most of the time, your instincts are correct.

DO NOT EDIT PREMATURELY

You may have trouble deciding what to change if you get bogged down checking commas, spelling, fragments, and the like. Such concerns as these are matters of correctness and are best dealt with later, during editing. During revision, focus on content, organization, and effective expression. Do not be distracted by editing concerns too early in the writing process.

DO NOT BE FOOLED BY APPEARANCES

Whether you write by hand or compose at the computer, you should revise a print copy of your draft at least once. But be aware: Typed material looks very professional because it is neat and well formatted; do not let that appearance fool you into thinking that no changes are needed.

Chapter Eleven

"Is It Cheating If Someone Helps Me?"

Of course it's cheating if someone else writes all or part of your paper or if you copy someone else's work and turn it in as your own. But that doesn't mean other people can't lend a hand. In fact, writers often seek feedback and ideas from other people. That's why you so often hear a writer say, "Read this and tell me what you think." Because the opinions of readers are so valuable to writers, this chapter explains strategies for securing helpful reader response.

Choose Your Readers Carefully

Choose readers who know the qualities of effective writing. A person who has never taken a writing course may not be a good choice. Also, use readers who are comfortable giving constructive criticism; do not use someone who is reluctant to tell you if something is wrong.

Give Your Readers a Legible Draft

Make your readers' job as easy as possible. If necessary, print out or write a fresh, clear copy of your draft so readers can easily read your work.

Give Your Readers Guidance

If you have specific concerns about your draft, mention them and ask your readers to speak to those points. Or give your readers a questionnaire like the one on the next page.

Reader Response Questionnaire

1. Can you easily tell what the thesis is? If so, what is that thesis?

   _____

   _____

2. Are you interested in reading about this thesis? Why or why not?

   _____

   _____

3. What do you like best about this essay?

   _____

   _____

4. Are any points unproven or unsupported? If so, which ones?

   _____

   _____

5. Is there anything you do not understand? If so, what?

   _____

   _____

6. Does the order of ideas make sense? If not, explain the problem.

   _____

   _____

7. Does any detail stray from the thesis? If so, what?

   _____

   _____

8. Does the introduction engage your interest? Why or why not?

   _____

   _____

9. Is the conclusion satisfying? Why or why not?

   _____

   _____

10. What advice do you have that was not covered by the previous questions?

   _____

   _____

GET MORE THAN ONE OPINION

Ask two or three reliable readers to respond to your draft, and then look for consensus. If a reader makes a comment you are unsure about, ask another reader to speak to that same point so you can have another opinion.

Follow the "Rule of Three"

If three readers have the same opinion, assume the opinion has merit. Seriously consider following their advice, unless your instructor tells you otherwise.

E-MAIL YOUR DRAFT

E-mail your draft to reliable readers to secure their reactions. If you want them to respond to particular sections of the draft, boldface those sections and ask your readers to pay particular attention to those parts. Many word processing programs allow inserting comments on the draft. Learn the procedure for inserting comments in your particular program.

POST ON FACEBOOK

After checking your privacy settings, post your draft on Facebook to get feedback from friends in your network. Or post part of your draft, the introduction perhaps, to get reader response on a particular part.

EVALUATE RESPONSES CAREFULLY

Readers are not always correct. Weigh their responses carefully. If you are unsure about the value of a response, ask your instructor or a writing center tutor. If you need clarification, ask your readers why they responded as they did.

DON'T TAKE CRITICISM PERSONALLY

Criticism can sting, but it can also be helpful. Try not to dismiss constructive criticism because you feel wounded. Remember, suggestions for improving your draft are about the writing task, not about you or your ability. No matter how well we write, each of us can learn from a sensitive reader.

BE A RELIABLE READER

If someone asks you to read and respond to a draft, be a reliable reader by remembering these points:

1. Read the entire draft to get an overview before you comment.
2. Give reasons for your reactions. Rather than saying, "I didn't like your conclusion," say, "I thought you stopped too suddenly in your conclusion."
3. If possible, suggest revisions, like this: "Your conclusion might be less abrupt if you explain why you were surprised by Jake's actions."
4. Note both strengths and weaknesses. If you note only problems, the writer might get discouraged; if you note only strengths, the writer won't know what to change.
5. Don't make too many comments, or you will overwhelm the writer. Focus on the most important revision issues.
6. Avoid commenting on grammar and usage, as these are editing concerns.

⚠ PLAGIARISM ALERT

It's perfectly ethical to get feedback from others and incorporate that feedback into your draft. However, you may not ask others to rewrite several sentences or one or more paragraphs and then incorporate that material into your writing. If you do that, you will be guilty of plagiarism. Thus, reliable readers can suggest a good word to use, an example that is telling, or an approach to your conclusion, but they cannot write for you.

CHAPTER TWELVE

"My Ideas Seem All Mixed Up."

There's nothing like finishing your first draft to boost your morale—that is, unless you read it over and everything is a jumble, and your ideas do not seem connected to each other. Does the jumble mean that your draft is no good? Absolutely not. It just means that you should use the suggestions in this chapter to better organize your writing.

USE TOPIC SENTENCES

A **topic sentence** presents the main idea of a paragraph. All the details in a paragraph must relate clearly and directly to that topic sentence (see page 13). If your ideas seem mixed up, check that you are using topic sentences to focus your body paragraphs. If you are not, add them. Then make sure that every sentence in each body paragraph relates to that topic sentence. If something does not relate directly, delete it, revise it, or move it to another paragraph where it fits better. If you compose at the computer, change each topic sentence to boldface to make checking easier.

WRITE A POSTDRAFT OUTLINE

Outline your draft *after* it is written to check the organization by filling in an outline map, outline tree, outline worksheet, or formal outline with the ideas already written in your draft. (See Chapter 3.) If points do not fit logically into a particular section of the outline, you have an organization problem that needs your attention.

If you compose at the computer, make a copy of your draft in a new file. Write your thesis at the top of the copy. Then identify the topic sentence and the major supporting details in each paragraph. Delete everything else from the essay, leaving just these sentences. Use roman and arabic numerals and capital and lowercase letters to create an outline from these sentences. Study this outline to be sure that every topic sentence relates to the thesis, that every supporting detail relates to its topic sentence, and that every detail follows logically from the one before it.

USE TRANSITIONS

Transitions are words and phrases that show how ideas relate to each other. Sometimes when your ideas seem mixed up, you just need to supply appropriate transitions to make the connections between points explicit. Consider these sentences:

Today's economy is not good for the stock market. There is still money to be made in speculative stocks.

Without a transitional word or phrase, the reader will not see how the ideas in the two sentences relate to each other. Add a transition to solve this problem:

Today's economy is not good for the stock market. <u>Nevertheless,</u> there is still money to be made in speculative stocks.

The following transitions can help you demonstrate how your ideas relate to each other:

also	for instance	in other words	next to
although	for this reason	in short	now
and	furthermore	in summary	on the contrary
as a result	however	in the same way	on the other hand
at the same time	in addition	indeed	similarly
consequently	in conclusion	later	then
earlier	in fact	moreover	therefore
even though	in front of	near	thus
for example	in like fashion	nevertheless	yet

REPEAT KEY WORDS

You can often show how ideas relate to each other by repeating a key word or words, like this:

The Senate is scheduled to vote on the tax reform <u>bill</u> Wednesday. This <u>bill</u> will reduce taxes.

 Use Synonyms

You can also demonstrate how ideas relate to each other by using synonyms to repeat an idea, like this:

The Senate is scheduled to vote on the tax reform <u>bill</u> Wednesday. This <u>legislation</u> will reduce taxes.

Use Outline Cards

Write your thesis and each of your main ideas on a separate index card. To experiment with alternative orders, arrange and rearrange the cards until your ideas progress in the best order. If you compose at the computer, make a copy of your draft in a new file. Then use the cut and paste functions to try your paragraphs in a new order.

Chapter Thirteen

❝My Draft Is Too Short.❞

Picture this: You think you have enough ideas to get under way, so you start drafting with enthusiasm and write all the way to the end. After placing your last period with a sense of satisfaction, you reread your work. But suddenly you don't feel so enthusiastic because you realize that your draft is much too short—and you've already said everything you can think of. What do you do? No, you do not throw yourself in front of a high-speed train. Instead, try some of the strategies in this chapter.

✳ Check Your Thesis

Study your thesis to see if it too much limits the territory you can cover. If so, broaden the thesis a bit so that you can cover more ground and thereby increase the length of your draft. Let's say that your draft has this thesis:

> *High school athletics teaches adolescents to be self-reliant.*

If you have exhausted everything you can say about how high school athletics teaches self-reliance, if you have tried all the techniques in this chapter, and if you still have only a page and a half of material, consider expanding your thesis to allow discussion of other points:

> *High school athletics teaches adolescents to be self-reliant. Interestingly, however, high school athletics also teaches students how to be team players.*

Now you can expand the draft by discussing two advantages of high school athletics rather than one.

A word of caution is in order: Do not get carried away when you expand your thesis, or you will be covering too much territory. Consider how difficult it would be to provide an adequately detailed discussion of this expanded thesis:

High school athletics teaches adolescents everything they need to know to succeed as adults: how to be self-reliant, how to be a team player, how to function under pressure, how to accept criticism, and how to give 100 percent.

An essay with this thesis will fail in one of two ways. Either it will be so long that the reader will feel overwhelmed, or it will provide only superficial treatment of the main points.

UNDERLINE MAJOR POINTS

Underline every major point in your draft. Then check to see how much you have written after each underlined point. If one underlined point is immediately followed by another underlined point, you have neglected to develop an idea. Adding supporting detail after one or more of your major points can solve your length problem. If you compose at the computer, place the cursor between your main points and their supporting details and hit the space bar five times to create a visual separation. The separation will help you study each point and its support individually to determine whether you should add details. (See Chapter 6 for ways to add supporting detail.)

SHOW AFTER YOU TELL

If your draft is too short, you may be *telling* your reader that things are true without *showing* that they are true. Remember to "show; don't just tell." Consider the following:

I have always hated winter. For one thing, the cold bothers me. For another, daily living becomes too difficult.

The previous sentences are an example of telling without showing. Here is a revision with detail added to *show:*

I have always hated winter. For one thing, the cold bothers me. Even in the house with the furnace running, I can never seem to get warm. I wear a turtleneck under a heavy wool sweater and drink one cup of hot tea after another in a futile effort to ease the chill that goes to my bones. A simple trip to the mailbox at the street leaves me chattering for an hour. My hands go numb, and my nose and ears sting from the cold. The doctor explained that I cannot tolerate the cold because I have a circulation problem that causes my capillaries to spasm, interrupting the blood flow to my extremities. I also hate winter because daily living becomes too difficult. Snow and ice are tracked into the house, necessitating frequent cleanups. Snow must be shoveled to get the car out of the driveway. Icy walks make walking treacherous, and driving to the grocery store becomes a dangerous endeavor thanks to slick, snow-covered roads.

✳ADD DESCRIPTION

Description can add interest and liveliness, and it can help your reader form clear mental images. To flesh out an essay, look for opportunities to describe a person or scene. For more on description, see page 50.

✳ADD EXAMPLES

Examples clarify matters and make things more specific. As you work to lengthen a draft, look for general statements that can be illustrated with a well-chosen example or two. For more on examples, see page 55.

✳ADD DIALOGUE

Sometimes you can enliven an essay by adding the words that were spoken. Consider the following paragraph:

> I stepped up to the plate, ready to swing away, but the catcher kept saying things to shake my confidence. I tried to ignore him and keep my focus, but the next thing I knew, I was too nervous to swing at all. The pitcher threw three pitches, the umpire called three strikes, and I walked to the dugout feeling like a fool.

Notice, now, how much more full-bodied the paragraph is with the addition of dialogue:

> I stepped up to the plate, ready to swing away, but the catcher kept saying things to shake my confidence. "I hope you don't choke like the last time," he sneered as I tapped the bat against the inside of my shoe. "Move in; easy out," he shouted to the outfield as I assumed my batting stance. I tried to ignore him and keep my focus, but the next thing I knew, I was too nervous to swing at all. "I figured you'd choke, you big baby," he cackled after the first called strike. The pitcher threw three pitches, the umpire called three strikes, and I walked to the dugout feeling like a fool.

✳EVALUATE THE SIGNIFICANCE OF AN IDEA

In addition to stating an idea, explain its importance, impact, or meaning. For example, assume you are arguing that the proposed site for the new state prison is not a good choice. You could explain the significance of the choice of site:

> The proposed site on the north end of town is favored by state legislators, not because it is inherently the best site, but because their wealthy campaign

contributors want the building as far away from their residences as possible. The legislators fear angering their wealthy supporters because they do not want to lose their financial assistance in future campaigns.

SHARE YOUR DRAFT WITH A RELIABLE READER

Ask someone with good judgment about writing to read your draft and suggest where and what kind of detail is needed. For more on using a reliable reader, see Chapter 11.

RETURN TO IDEA GENERATION

Your draft may be too short because you did not generate enough ideas to write about. If you have a favorite idea generation technique, try it now. If it lets you down, try one or more of the other techniques described in Chapter 1.

USE YOUR COMPUTER'S TOOLS

Many word processing programs allow you to do a word count, which is helpful if your instructor has designated a minimum number of words for your writing. Use this function to determine how close you are to the required length. In addition, you can highlight individual paragraphs to count the number of words in each one.

Your computer will also allow you to use the page or print layout function so you can see each page of your draft on the screen. With this view, you can identify your shortest paragraphs and target them for additional development.

AVOID PADDING

When you add detail, do not state the obvious or give unrelated or unnecessary information, or you will be guilty of **padding**—writing useless material just to bulk up the piece.

Assume that you are explaining how schools foster competition, rather than cooperation, in students. If you say that schools have students compete for grades, compete for positions on sports teams, compete for student government, compete for scholarships, and compete for cheerleading, you would be providing helpful examples to illustrate your point. However, if you give a dictionary definition of *competition* as "the act of struggling to win some prize, honor, or advantage," you would be padding your essay with unnecessary information.

CHAPTER FOURTEEN

"My Draft Is Too Long."

Perhaps you are inspired and write page after page after page after page—all the while feeling great because you have so much to say. Unfortunately, longer is not necessarily better. Your reader's time is valuable, so keep your writing to the assigned length or to a length that will not unduly tax your audience. If your draft is too long, try the strategies given here.

CHECK YOUR THESIS

If you have been assigned to write an essay of 1,000 words, and your draft comes in at 2,000 words, try to narrow the scope of your thesis. If it takes in too much territory, you will have to cover too many points, and the result will be a very long piece of writing. Consider this thesis:

The amount of violence on television, in the movies, and in popular fiction is alarming.

Discussing television, movie, and book violence in adequate detail would require many, many pages. A shorter, more manageable essay would result from a thesis like this:

The amount of violence on prime-time network television is alarming.

ELIMINATE UNNECESSARY POINTS

Avoid making unnecessary points. For example, assume you are writing a report on the mutual funds that provide the best retirement income. If you are writing for your boss, who is an investment banker, you need not define the term *mutual funds*. However, in a newspaper article for readers who may not know what mutual funds are, a definition would be helpful. Similarly, if you are comparing two kinds of bicycles, you should not mention that both have two tires; doing so would be stating the obvious. If you work at the computer, cut and paste what you delete into a "scraps" file. You may be able to use the material in later writings.

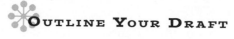

OUTLINE YOUR DRAFT

Even if you outlined before drafting, outline your draft after you write it. Then check the outline to be sure you are not repeating points, stating the obvious, or including irrelevant detail.

ELIMINATE WORDINESS

Eliminate wordiness in the following ways:

1. Eliminate repetition.

Wordy   My biggest problem and concern was how to pay next month's rent. (Problem and concern are repetitious.)

Better   My biggest problem was how to pay next month's rent.

Better   My biggest concern was how to pay next month's rent.

2. Eliminate **deadwood** (words that add no meaning).

Deadwood	Better
the color green	green
mix together	mix
past history	past
end result	result
important essentials	essentials

Wordy   I cannot concentrate unless I am alone by myself.

Better   I cannot concentrate unless I am alone.

Better   I cannot concentrate unless I am by myself.

3. Pare down wordy phrases.

Wordy	Better
in this day and age	now
in society today	today
being that	since
due to the fact that	because
for the purpose of	so

Wordy   At this point in time, I do not think we can afford the rate increase.

Better   I do not think we can afford the rate increase now.

4. Reduce the number of phrases.

Wordy   The shortage <u>of skilled labor in this country</u> points to the need <u>for a greater number of vocational education programs</u>.

Better   This country's skilled labor shortage points to a needed increase in vocational education programs.

5. Reduce the number of "that" clauses.

Wordy   The reporters asked the senator to repeat the explanation <u>that she gave earlier</u>.

Better   The reporters asked the senator to repeat her earlier explanation.

6. Eliminate the unnecessary qualifiers *some, very, quite, I think, in my opinion,* and *it seems to me* when these add no important meaning.

Wordy   The air was quite stifling. Smith, it seems to me, is the better candidate.

Better   The air was stifling. Smith is the better candidate.

Do Not Overwrite Your Introduction or Conclusion

Be sure your introduction and conclusion are not unduly long. These paragraphs are meant only to pave the way for your main discussion and tie things off at the end.

Use Your Computer's Tools

Hit the enter key after each sentence to reformat your writing into a list of sentences. With your sentences listed, you may find it easier to check for wordiness. You can also use the search/find function to locate these often unnecessary words: *very, some, quite, so.* If you judge they should be cut, do so.

CHAPTER FIFTEEN

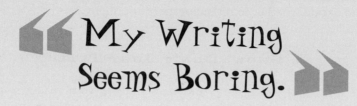

"My Writing Seems Boring."

I couldn't put it down!" "A real page-turner!" "A must read!" No, these are not the exclamations people must make about your writing, but you do have a responsibility to hold your reader's interest. If your draft seems boring, try the strategies described in this chapter to punch up your detail and style.

✳ REPLACE GENERAL WORDS WITH SPECIFIC ONES

To add interest, replace general words with more specific ones. Here are two sentences. The first has general words, which are underlined; the second has specific words, which are also underlined. Which sentence is more interesting?

General words The <u>car went</u> down the <u>street</u>.
Specific words The <u>red Corvette streaked</u> down <u>Dover Avenue</u>.

You probably found the second sentence more interesting because of its more specific word choice.

The following chart will give you a clearer idea of the difference between general and specific words:

General	Specific	General	Specific
car	1989 Buick	dog	mangy collie
sweater	yellow cardigan	hat	Phillies cap
shoes	Nike Air Max	speak	mumble
feel good	feel optimistic	book	*The Help*
walk	saunter	drink	slurp
cry	sob loudly	said	snapped
house	two-story colonial	rain	pounding rain
a lot	nine	later	in two days

If you compose at the computer, you can use the search/find function to locate these general words: *very, quite, a lot, rather, really, great, good, bad,* and *some.* Evaluate each and decide whether to revise for more specificity.

SHOW, DON'T JUST TELL

To energize a draft, follow general sentences that *tell* your reader something is true with specific ones that *show* that it is true. In the following example, the first sentence tells and the second sentence shows.

> The child seemed sad. He moped around the house all day, refusing to play with his favorite action figures and showing no interest in his favorite foods, not even chocolate chip cookies.

USE ACTIVE VOICE

To give your writing more energy, write sentences so that their subjects perform the actions indicated by the verbs. Then your sentences will be in the **active voice.** Here is an example:

> The labor leader negotiated a new contract for the autoworkers. (The action suggested by the verb <u>negotiated</u> is performed by the subject, <u>labor leader</u>.)

When the subject does not perform the verb's action (putting the sentence in the **passive voice**), the sentence has less energy:

> The new contract for the autoworkers was negotiated by the labor leader. (The subject <u>the new contract</u> does not perform the action of the verb <u>negotiated</u>.)

SUBSTITUTE ACTION VERBS FOR FORMS OF *TO BE*

Forms of *to be (am, is, are, was, were)* have less energy and interest than action verbs, so when possible use action verbs, like this:

Less energy   Mayor Daley <u>was</u> always a believer in party politics.

More energy   Mayor Daley always <u>believed</u> in party politics.

REWRITE CLICHÉS

Clichés are tired, overworked expressions. At one time the expressions were fresh and interesting, but with overuse, they have become boring. Here is a representative sampling of clichés:

cold as ice	free as a bird	sadder but wiser
high as a kite	last but not least	green with envy
fresh as a daisy	stiff as a board	hard as nails
under the weather	bull in a china shop	raining cats and dogs
in the same boat	the last straw	smart as a whip

To add interest, replace clichés with more original phrasings.

Cliché   When the police officer pulled me over for speeding, I was <u>shaking like a leaf</u>.

Revision   When the police officer pulled me over for speeding, I was <u>trembling with anxiety</u>.

ELIMINATE OBVIOUS STATEMENTS

Stating the obvious makes writing boring. Assume you are arguing that young people should not be permitted to watch more than an hour of television a day. A sentence like the following will bore a reader because some of what it says is so obvious it does not need to be said at all:

Television, an electronic device for bringing sound and pictures into the home, can be a positive or negative influence on our children, depending on how it is used.

To make your writing more interesting, eliminate obvious statements:

Television can influence our children for good or ill, depending on how it is used.

INCLUDE DIALOGUE

Including the words people spoke can enliven writing, especially when you are telling a story, because dialogue adds interest and immediacy. For more on dialogue, see page 88.

ADD DESCRIPTION

Description adds vitality and interest, so look for opportunities to describe something: a scene, a person's clothing, a facial expression, a tone of voice, the brightness of the sun, the feel of a handshake. The description need not be elaborate, nor should it distract the reader from your main point. For example, if you are telling the story of a first encounter, some description can add liveliness, like this:

The door was open, and I saw Dr. Harkness hunched over his desk, his nose on the paper he was studying, his eyes squinted into slits. I knocked on the door frame to get his attention, but the barely perceptible sound was too much for him. He jerked upright, startled by the intrusion. When he saw me, he brushed wisps of white hair from his eyes, smoothed his red and blue flannel shirt, and smiled sheepishly. "How can I help you, young man?" he asked, as he lifted his bulky frame from the chair.

✳ ADD EXAMPLES

Examples add interest because they are specific, so look for opportunities to follow a general point with an example. For instance, if you say that Lee is a scatterbrain, show this by giving the example of the time Lee locked the keys in the car three times in one day.

✳ TELL A STORY

A brief story can add interest and help establish a point by serving as an example. For instance, assume you are explaining that being a student *and* a parent can get very complicated. Also assume that one point you make is that the two roles can conflict with each other. To establish this point, you could tell the story of the time your six-year-old woke up sick three hours before your history exam and you had to get her to the doctor, arrange for a babysitter, pick up a prescription—and still make it to class on time.

✳ CHECK YOUR THESIS

If your thesis takes in too much territory, you can be forced into a superficial, general discussion—and such discussions are boring. For example, consider this thesis:

Professional sports should be reformed.

An essay that adequately covers all professional sports and all areas that could benefit from reform is likely to involve a superficial discussion because anything in-depth will lead to a very long piece. If your thesis is too ambitious, pare it down, like this:

During the off-season as well as the playing season, athletes should have to submit to random drug testing.

Now you can provide a much more interesting discussion by giving specifics and still have a piece that is of manageable length.

✳ USE YOUR COMPUTER'S STYLE CHECK CAUTIOUSLY

If your word processing program includes a style check that flags problems, use it with caution, as these checks are not always reliable. Do not automatically assume that a flagged passage is really a problem—evaluate it yourself. Conversely, do not assume that unflagged passages are problem-free.

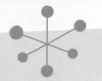

Chapter Sixteen

"My Writing Sounds Choppy."

Read this paragraph out loud. It sounds choppy. It does not flow. The style seems immature. It sounds like it was written by someone's kid brother. This is my way of showing that choppiness is bad. Is it working?

Actually, you do not always have to read your work aloud to detect choppiness. When you read silently, the words "sound" in your brain, allowing you to "hear" this problem. Then you can eliminate it with the techniques described in this chapter.

Use Different Sentence Openers

When too many sentences in a row begin the same way, writing sounds choppy. For example, the first paragraph of this chapter sounds choppy because most of the sentences begin with the subject. The solution is to mix the following sentence openings.

1. Open with a descriptive word (a *modifier*).

    Strangely, little Billy did not enjoy his birthday.

    Confused, the stranger asked directions to a bus stop.

    Melting, the ice formed slushy puddles on the pavement.

2. Open with a descriptive phrase (a *modifier*).

    Despite my better judgment, I bought a ticket for the roller coaster ride.

    Hiding in the living room, nine of us waited for the right moment to leap out and yell, "Surprise!"

Pleased by her grade on the physics exam, Loretta treated herself to a special dinner.

Under the couch, the wet dog hid from her owner.

3. Open with a *dependent clause* (a word group with a subject and verb that cannot stand alone as a sentence).

When Congress announced its budget reform package, members of both political parties offered their support.

If the basketball team can recruit a power forward, we will have all the ingredients for a winning season.

Before you contribute to a charity, check the identification of the person requesting the money.

4. Open with *to* and the verb (an *infinitive*).

To protect our resources, we must all recycle.

To convince my parents to buy me a car, I had to agree to pay the car insurance.

To gain five pounds by the start of wrestling season, Luis doubled his intake of carbohydrates.

5. Open with the subject.

Losses led gains in today's stock market activity.

Corvina's goal is to become the youngest manager in the company's history.

The curtains were dulled by years of accumulated dirt.

If you compose at the computer, you can copy your writing into a new file. Then hit the return key after each sentence to turn that writing into a list. With sentences separated in this way, you can more easily determine whether too many sentences are the same length or open the same way.

❋ VARY THE PLACEMENT OF TRANSITIONS

Transitions are words and phrases that link ideas and show how they relate to each other. (Transitions are discussed on page 84.) One way to eliminate choppiness is to vary the placement of transitions.

Transition at the beginning	In addition, providing child care in the workplace is a good idea because half of all mothers now work.
Transition in the middle	Jan's opinion, on the other hand, is that child care programs will cost too much.
Transition at the end	Many employers now offer day care as a benefit, however.

✳ COMBINE SHORT SENTENCES

When you hear choppiness, look to see if you have two or more short sentences in a row. If so, combine at least two of those short sentences into a longer one, using one of these words:

and	or	for	yet
but	nor	so	because

Short sentences (choppy)	The house was well constructed. It was decorated badly.
Combined sentence (smoother)	The house was well constructed, but it was deco rated badly.
Short sentences (choppy)	The police and firefighters both needed money. They combined their resources in a fund-raiser.
Combined sentence (smoother)	The police and firefighters both needed money, so they combined their resources in a fund-raiser.

✳ ALTERNATE LONG AND SHORT SENTENCES

The following examples alternate long and short sentences. As you read them, notice how well they flow.

Short followed by long	The coach jumped to his feet. Although he had been coaching for 20 years, he had never before seen such a perfectly executed play.
Long followed by short	This city needs a mayor who knows how to deal effectively with the city council and how to trim waste from the municipal budget. This city needs Dale Davidson.

✳ USE PARALLEL CONSTRUCTIONS

So sentences flow smoothly, keep series items **parallel** by putting them in the same grammatical form.

Not parallel	Coach Rico values <u>teamwork</u>, <u>sportsmanship</u>, and <u>she values effort</u>.
Parallel	Coach Rico values <u>teamwork</u>, <u>sportsmanship</u>, and <u>effort</u>.
Not parallel	The offensive television commercial <u>insults women</u>, <u>glamorizes drinking</u>, and <u>it diminishes the importance of the family</u>.
Parallel	The offensive television commercial <u>insults women</u>, <u>glamorizes drinking</u>, and <u>diminishes the importance of the family</u>.

Your word processing program's style check may flag possible parallelism problems. However, style checks are not completely reliable, so do not assume that a flagged sentence has a problem—or that an unflagged sentence is satisfactory.

USE YOUR EAR

Read your writing aloud with a pen in your hand. When you hear choppiness, place a check mark. Then go back and try the techniques described in this chapter to improve the flow of sentences.

PART IV

A Troubleshooting Guide to Editing

Everyone—and I mean *everyone*—makes mistakes with grammar, spelling, punctuation, and capitalization. There is nothing wrong with making mistakes—as long as *you* find and correct them in a process called **editing**. Editing is important because mistakes are distracting, and serious errors or frequent mistakes can cause readers to lose confidence in your ability.

✳ TROUBLESHOOTING STRATEGIES

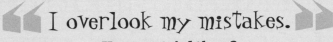

❝❝ I overlook my mistakes. ❞❞

Have you tried these?

❏ Walking away (p. 104) ❏ Using a checklist (p. 106)

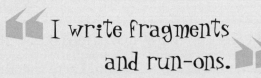

❝❝ I write fragments and run-ons. ❞❞

Have you tried these?

❏ Reading backward (p. 109) ❏ Studying sentences individually (p. 114)

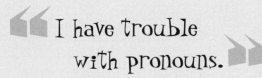

❝❝ I have trouble with pronouns. ❞❞

Have you tried these?

❏ Crossing out (p. 116 and p. 117) ❏ Circling *who* and *whom* (p. 119)

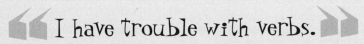

❝❝ I have trouble with verbs. ❞❞

Have you tried these?

❏ Crossing out (p. 122) ❏ Rewriting questions (p. 123)

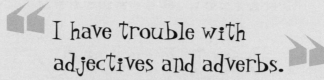

I have trouble with adjectives and adverbs.

Have you tried these?

- ❏ Distinguishing adjectives from adverbs **(p. 127)**
- ❏ Checking *-ing* openers **(p. 129)**

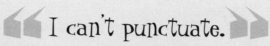

I can't punctuate.

Have you tried these?

- ❏ Checking before the subject **(p. 131)**
- ❏ Identifying missing letters **(p. 136)**

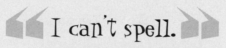

I can't spell.

Have you tried these?

- ❏ Looking for prefixes **(p. 144)**
- ❏ Using memory tricks **(p. 145)**

CHAPTER SEVENTEEN

"I Don't Find My Mistakes."

When your teacher or other reader finds a mistake that you overlooked, do you smack yourself on the forehead and ask, "How did I miss that?" The techniques in this chapter and the ones that follow can help you find and correct errors you might otherwise overlook.

✳ EDIT LAST

The time to **edit** (find and correct mistakes) is near the end of your writing process. Editing during idea generation, drafting, and revising is inefficient because you may look up the spelling of a word that you eliminate during revision or check a comma in a sentence that never makes it to the final draft. However, once done with revising, you can scrutinize your draft for errors.

✳ LEAVE YOUR WORK FOR A WHILE

By the time you are ready to look for errors, you may not have a fresh enough perspective to notice mistakes, so leave your writing for a day to clear your head. When you return, you will have a sharper eye for spotting errors.

✳ POINT TO EACH WORD AND PUNCTUATION MARK

Go over your writing very slowly. If you build up even a little speed, you can overlook errors because you will see what you *intended* to write rather than what you actually *did* write. One way to ensure that you move slowly is to point to each word and punctuation mark and study each one a second or two. Read what you are pointing to; do not move your finger or pen ahead of what you are reading, or you will build up speed and miss mistakes.

Isolate Each Line

Place a ruler under the first line of your writing and examine that line for mistakes one word at a time. Then drop the ruler down a line and examine that line for mistakes. This way, you may have better luck finding errors because you are less likely to build up speed and miss mistakes. Also, the ruler prevents the words below the line from entering your visual field and distracting you. If you compose at the computer, reformat your draft with four spaces between each line to narrow your visual field. When done editing, restore your original spacing.

Prepare a Fresh, Typed Copy

You can often spot errors more easily in type. Also, you can be more objective about typed copy because it seems more like printed material—more like someone else's writing.

Reformat Your Draft

If you drafted at the computer, copy the draft into a new file and then change the font size and type to give your writing a new appearance. For example, if you used Times New Roman, size 12, try using Calibri, size 14 and boldface the type. When your draft looks significantly different, you may spot errors more readily.

Listen to Your Draft

Sometimes you can hear mistakes that you overlook visually. Have someone read your draft to you, read it aloud to yourself, or speak it into a recorder and play back the audio. If you speak your draft, be sure to read *exactly* what is on the page. Remember, writers tend to read what they *meant* to say rather than what they *did* say. Also, remember that some mistakes, such as misspellings, cannot be heard, so listening should be combined with visual editing.

Learn Your Pattern of Error

We all make mistakes, but we do not all make the *same* mistakes. One person may misspell words often, another may write run-on sentences, another may have trouble choosing the correct verb, and so on. Know the kinds of mistakes you make, so you can make a special effort to locate those errors.

Once you know the kinds of mistakes you make, you may also determine under what circumstances you make them. For example, once you discover that you have trouble choosing verbs, a little study of your writing may tell you that you have this trouble whenever you begin a sentence with *there is* or *there are*. This is valuable information because it tells you to check the verbs in any sentences that begin with these words.

If you compose at the computer, you can use your search/find function to locate trouble spots. For example, if you habitually misuse semicolons and confuse *affect* and *effect*, find every semicolon, *affect*, and *effect* in your draft and check your usage.

✳ USE AN EDITING CHECKLIST

An editing checklist can ensure that you are attending to everything. Use the one below or devise your own checklist of errors you often make. If you compose at the computer, split your screen, and place your editing checklist in one window and your draft in the other. Consult the checklist as you edit.

NOTE: The page numbers in parentheses refer to helpful pages in this book.

1. Have you read your work aloud to listen for problems? (page 105)
2. Did you check every possible misspelling in a dictionary or with a spell checker? (page 143)
3. Did you edit for run-on sentences and comma splices? (page 113)
4. Did you edit for sentence fragments? (page 108)
5. Did you check your verbs? (page 122)
6. Did you check your pronouns? (page 116)
7. Did you check your modifiers? (page 127)
8. Have you checked your punctuation? (pages 131, 134, and 136)
9. Have you checked your capital letters? (page 140)

✳ TRUST YOUR INSTINCTS

Maybe you have had this experience: You have a feeling that something is wrong. However, you cannot give the problem a name, and you are not sure how to solve it, so you skip it and hope for the best. Then you submit your writing, and sure enough—your reader was troubled by the same thing you were troubled by. If you have had this experience, you have learned that your instincts are reliable. Because much of what you know about language has been internalized, an inner alarm may sound when you have made a mistake. Always heed that alarm, even if you are not sure what the problem is or how to solve it. Get help, if necessary, for diagnosing and eliminating the error.

✳ Edit More Than Once

Many writers edit once for anything they can find and a separate time for each of the kinds of errors they tend to make. If you compose at the computer, edit both on the screen and on a paper copy. Be sure to transfer all your paper edits to your computer copy.

✳ When in Doubt, Check It Out

When you are unsure about something, look it up in a grammar handbook. If you do not own one, check one out of your campus library or purchase one in your college bookstore.

✳ Learn the Rules

You cannot edit confidently if you do not know the rules. Many people think the grammar and usage rules can be understood only by English teachers, but the truth is that anyone can learn them. Invest in a grammar handbook, and each time you make an error, learn the appropriate rule.

✳ Get Help

Ask someone to go over your writing to find mistakes that you overlooked. Be sure, however, that the person who helps you edit is someone who knows grammar and usage rules, or you will not get reliable information. If your school has a writing center, stop in there for reliable editing assistance. Remember, though, that the ultimate responsibility for editing is yours. You must learn and apply the rules on your own, with only backup help from others.

✳ Use Your Computer's Grammar Check with Caution

Your computer's grammar check gets many things right, but it is not always correct. It overlooks many errors and flags some errors incorrectly, so evaluate its flags and suggestions carefully.

CHAPTER EIGHTEEN

"I Used a Period and a Capital Letter, so Why Isn't This a Sentence?"

You can put a saddle on a donkey, but that won't make it a horse. Similarly, you can start a word group with a capital letter and end it with a period, question mark, or exclamation point, but that won't necessarily make it a sentence.

UNDERSTAND WHAT A SENTENCE FRAGMENT IS

If you capitalize and punctuate a word group that cannot be a sentence as if it *were* a sentence, you have written a **sentence fragment**.

Word group that cannot be a sentence	then fell asleep
Sentence fragment	The child rolled over. <u>Then fell asleep</u>.
Correction	The child rolled over. Then he fell asleep.
Word group that cannot be a sentence	although the election was close
Sentence fragment	<u>Although the election was close</u>. The losing candidate did not ask for a recount.
Correction	Although the election was close, the losing candidate did not ask for a recount.
Word group that cannot be a sentence	such as loyalty, creativity, and integrity
Sentence fragment	Maria has many admirable traits. <u>Such as loyalty, creativity, and integrity</u>.
Correction	Maria has many admirable traits, such as loyalty, creativity, and integrity.

🟡 LOOK FOR SUBJECTS AND COMPLETE VERBS

Check each word group you are calling a sentence to be sure that each has a subject and a complete verb. If one or both of these is missing, you have a sentence fragment.

Missing subject fragment Katrina cashed her first paycheck. <u>Then began planning a vacation.</u>

Incomplete verb fragment <u>The storm heading east quickly.</u> It will cause severe flooding.

Missing subject and verb fragment <u>By ten o'clock this morning.</u> The tide will be low enough to look for shells.

🟡 ISOLATE AND READ

If your draft is relatively short, start at the beginning and place one finger of your left hand under the capital letter. Then place a finger of your right hand under the period, question mark, or exclamation point. Now read the word group between your fingers. If it sounds as if something is missing or if the word group cannot stand alone as a sentence, you probably have a sentence fragment.

If you compose at the computer, you can isolate text by pressing the enter key before each capital letter marking a sentence beginning. Doing this will reformat your writing into a list of word groups you are calling sentences. With word groups isolated this way, you may find it easier to edit for fragments. Of course, after editing, be sure to return your paper to its original format.

TIP: Some people have more success if they read the word groups out loud.

🟡 READ YOUR DRAFT BACKWARD

Read your last sentence; pause for a moment to consider whether the word group can be a sentence. Then read the next-to-the-last sentence, again pausing to consider. Proceed this way until you have worked back to the first sentence.

🟡 CHECK *-ING* AND *-ED* VERB FORMS

Sometimes sentence fragments result when *-ing* or *-ed* verb forms stand by themselves, without an accompanying verb. Here are two examples with the *-ing* and *-ed* verb forms underlined:

Fragment The kittens <u>stretching</u> after their naps.

Fragment The child <u>frustrated</u> by the complicated toy.

To correct fragments that result when *-ing* or *-ed* verbs stand alone, pick an appropriate verb from this list and add it to the *-ing* or *-ed* form:

is   was   have   had
are   were   has

Fragment	The kittens <u>stretching</u> after their naps.
Sentence	The kittens <u>are stretching</u> after their naps.
Sentence	The kittens <u>were stretching</u> after their naps.
Fragment	The child <u>frustrated</u> by the complicated toy.
Sentence	The child <u>is frustrated</u> by the complicated toy.
Sentence	The child <u>was frustrated</u> by the complicated toy.

To find fragments that result when *-ing* or *-ed* verbs stand alone, go through your draft checking each *-ing* and *-ed* verb form. Read the sentence with the form and ask if a verb from the above list is necessary. Sometimes, as in the following example, an *-ed* verb *can* stand alone:

Sentence	The kittens <u>stretched</u> after their naps.

✳ CHECK FOR FRAGMENT WARNING WORDS

The following words often begin sentence fragments:

after	before	such as
although	especially	unless
as	even though	until
as if	for example	when
as long as	if	whenever
as soon as	in order to	where
as though	since	wherever
because	so that	while

Check every word group that begins with one of the above words or phrases. (If you compose at the computer, you can use the search/find function to locate the warning words.) However, do not assume that anything beginning with one of these words is automatically a sentence fragment because sentences, too, can begin with these words and phrases. To be sure, read aloud to hear whether the words can stand alone as a sentence.

Sentence	While Rudy cleaned the house, Sue cooked dinner.
Fragment	While Rudy cleaned the house. Sue cooked dinner.

❋ Watch Out for *Who*, *Whom*, *Whose*, *Which*, and *Where*

If you begin a word group with *who, whom, whose, which,* or *where* without asking a question, you most likely have written a sentence fragment.

Sentence	Who lives next door?
Fragment	Who lives next door.
Sentence	Whose advice have I valued over the years?
Fragment	Whose advice I have valued over the years.

Look at any word group that begins with *who, whom, whose, which,* or *where*. (You can use your computer's search/find function to locate *who, whom, whose, which,* and *where*.) If it is not asking a question, join the word group to the sentence before it.

Sentence and fragment	Stavros is a good friend. <u>Whose advice I have valued over the years</u>.
Sentence	Stavros is a good friend, whose advice I have valued over the years.

❋ Eliminate the Fragments

The previous techniques will help you locate sentence fragments; the next two techniques will help you eliminate fragments once you find them. No one technique will work for every fragment, so if one correction method does not work, try the other.

Join the Fragment to a Sentence before or after It

Sentence and fragment	The custom of hat-tipping goes back to the knights. <u>Who would remove their helmets before a lord</u>.
Fragment joined to sentence	The custom of hat-tipping goes back to the knights, who would remove their helmets before a lord.
Fragment and sentence	<u>While trying on the cashmere sweater</u>. Molly snagged the sleeve with her class ring.
Fragment joined to sentence	While trying on the cashmere sweater, Molly snagged the sleeve with her class ring.

Add the Missing Word or Words

To eliminate a fragment that results when a subject or all or part of the verb is left out, add the missing word or words.

Sentence and fragment	The auto mechanic assured us the repairs would be minor. <u>Then proceeded to list a dozen things wrong with the car.</u>
Fragment eliminated with addition of the missing subject *he*	The auto mechanic assured us the repairs would be minor. Then he proceeded to list a dozen things wrong with the car.
Fragment	The Surgeon General announcing new nutritional guidelines.
Fragment eliminated with addition of the missing part of the verb *is*	The Surgeon General is announcing new nutritional guidelines.
Sentence and fragment	Police chiefs want to hire more officers. <u>However, not without additional funds.</u>
Fragment eliminated with addition of the missing subject and verb	Police chiefs want to hire more officers. However, they cannot do so without additional funds.

CHAPTER NINETEEN

"How Can This Be a Run-On or a Comma Splice? It's Not Even Long."

I f you have a tendency to write run-on sentences or comma splices, you are in very good company. They are two of the most frequently occurring writing errors.

UNDERSTAND WHAT RUN-ON SENTENCES AND COMMA SPLICES ARE

A **run-on sentence** occurs when two word groups that can be sentences **(independent clauses)** stand together without any separation. A **comma splice** occurs when two word groups that can be sentences (independent clauses) stand together with only a comma between them. Run-on sentences and comma splices create confusion because they blur the points where sentences begin and end.

Independent clause   Charleston Harbor is a fascinating place to visit

Independent clause   many historical attractions are there

A *run-on sentence* is created when these independent clauses are not separated:

Run-on sentence   Charleston Harbor is a fascinating place to visit many historical attractions are there.

A *comma splice* is created when two independent clauses are separated by nothing more than a comma:

Comma splice   Charleston Harbor is a fascinating place to visit, many historical attractions are there.

❋UNDERSTAND HOW TO SEPARATE INDEPENDENT CLAUSES

You can separate independent clauses three ways:

1. **With a comma and coordinating conjunction** *(and, but, or, nor, for, so, yet)*
   Charleston Harbor is a fascinating place to visit⟨ for⟩many historical attractions are there.

2. **With a semicolon (;)**
   Charleston Harbor is a fascinating place to visit⟨;⟩many historical attractions are there.

3. **With a period and a capital letter**
   Charleston Harbor is a fascinating place to visit⟨M⟩any historical attractions are there.

❋CORRECT RUN-ONS AND COMMA SPLICES WITH DEPENDENT CLAUSES

To eliminate a run-on or comma splice, turn one of the independent clauses into a **dependent clause** (a word group that has a subject and a verb but cannot stand as a sentence).

Run-on sentence   Charleston Harbor is a fascinating place to visit many historical attractions are there.

Comma splice   Charleston Harbor is a fascinating place to visit, many historical attractions are there.

Correction   Because many historical attractions are there, Charleston Harbor is a fascinating place to visit.

❋STUDY SENTENCES INDIVIDUALLY

If your draft is not long, study each of your sentences separately. Place one finger of your left hand under the capital letter and one finger of your right hand under the end mark of punctuation. Then identify the number of independent clauses (word groups that can stand as sentences) between your fingers. If you have one, the sentence is fine. If you have two or more, be sure you separate the independent clauses as explained in this chapter.

If you compose at the computer, you can isolate text by pressing the enter key before each capital letter beginning a sentence to reformat your writing into a list of word groups you are calling sentences. With word groups isolated this way, you may find it easier to edit for run-ons and comma splices. Of course, after editing, be sure to return your paper to its original format.

✳ UNDERLINE WARNING WORDS

Pay special attention to these words because they often begin independent clauses (word groups that can be sentences):

as a result	furthermore	moreover	similarly
consequently	hence	nevertheless	then
finally	however	next	therefore
for example	in addition	on the contrary	thus

Underline any of these warning words in your draft, or use your computer's search/find function to locate them. Check what is on *both sides* of each underlined word. If—and only if—an independent clause is on *both sides,* place a semicolon (not a comma) before the warning word.

✳ FORGET ABOUT LONG AND SHORT

Many people think that a long sentence is sure to be a run-on or comma splice and that a short sentence cannot possibly be one. However, length is not a factor. The only factor is how independent clauses are separated.

CHAPTER TWENTY

"It Is I; It Is Me— What's the Difference?"

There you are writing along, and then it happens—you have to use a pronoun, and you are not sure which one is correct: Did the police officer issue the warning to Lee and me or to Lee and I? "Lee and me; no, it's Lee and I; no, wait, Lee and me." Ah, what the heck—you pick one and hope for the best. If you stumble over pronouns, the procedures in this chapter can help.

CROSS OUT EVERYTHING IN THE PHRASE BUT THE PRONOUN

When a pronoun is joined with a noun, you may be unsure which pronoun to use. Is it "Luis and I" or "Luis and me"? Is it "the girls and us" or "the girls and we"? To decide, cross out everything in the phrase but the pronoun and read what is left:

~~My brother and~~ I saw the movie six times.

~~My brother and~~ me saw the movie six times.

With everything but the pronoun crossed out, you can more easily tell that the correct choice is *I:*

My brother and I saw the movie six times.

Here is another example:

Dr. Cohen lent ~~Maria and~~ I a copy of the book.

Dr. Cohen lent ~~Maria and~~ me a copy of the book.

With everything but the pronoun crossed out, you can more easily tell that the correct choice is *me:*

Dr. Cohen lent Maria and me a copy of the book.

✳ CROSS OUT WORDS THAT RENAME

Sometimes words follow a pronoun and rename it.

We baseball players	Baseball players follows the pronoun and renames it.
Us sophomores	Sophomores follows the pronoun and renames it.
You sports fans	Sports fans follows the pronoun and renames it.

To choose the correct pronoun, cross out the words that rename:

We ~~spectators~~ jumped to our feet and cheered when the band took the field.

Us ~~spectators~~ jumped to our feet and cheered when the band took the field.

With the renaming word crossed out, the correct choice is clearer:

We spectators jumped to our feet and cheered when the band took the field.

Here is another example:

Loud rock music can be irritating to we ~~older folks~~.

Loud rock music can be irritating to us ~~older folks~~.

With the renaming words crossed out, the correct choice is clearer:

Loud rock music can be irritating to us older folks.

✳ ADD THE MISSING WORDS IN COMPARISONS

Which is it: "Bev is a better foul shooter than I" or "Bev is a better foul shooter than me"? To find out, add the unstated word:

Bev is a better foul shooter than I am.

Bev is a better foul shooter than me am.

With the missing word added, you can tell that the correct pronoun is *I*:

Bev is a better foul shooter than I.

Here is another example:

John Grisham's new novel interested Miguel as much as I.

John Grisham's new novel interested Miguel as much as me.

To decide on the correct pronoun, add the missing words:

John Grisham's new novel interested Miguel as much as it interested I.

John Grisham's new novel interested Miguel as much as it interested me.

With the missing comparison words added, you can tell that the correct pronoun is *me*.

✳ USE *THEY*, *THEIR*, AND *THEM* WITH PLURAL NOUNS

They, their, and *them* refer to plural nouns:

All students should bring(their)notebooks to the next class; if(they)forget(them) class partici-
pation will be difficult.

A problem occurs when *they, their,* or *them* is used to refer to a singular noun:

A person who cares about the environment will recycle.(They)will also avoid using Styrofoam and plastic.

In the previous sentence the plural *they* refers to the singular *person,* creating a
problem called **lack of agreement in number.** To eliminate the problem, make
the pronoun and noun agree in one of these two ways:

Singular noun and singular pronoun A person who cares about the environment will recycle.(He or she)will also avoid using Styrofoam and plastic.

Plural noun and plural pronoun People who care about the environment will recycle.
(They)will also avoid using Styrofoam and plastic.

To ensure agreement in number, check *they, their,* and *them* (you can use your
computer's search/find function) to be sure each of these pronouns refers to a plural
noun. If it does not, make the noun plural or change the pronoun to a singular form.

✳ REMEMBER THAT THE *-BODY, -ONE,* AND *-THING* WORDS ARE SINGULAR

In formal usage, *anybody, everybody, nobody, somebody, anyone, everyone, no one, someone, anything, everything, nothing,* and *something* (the **indefinite pronouns**) are
singular. Therefore, the words that refer to them should also be singular.

Everybody should remember(his or her)admission forms when reporting to orientation.
Someone left(his or her)coat in the auditorium.
Anybody who wants to bring(his or her)family may do so.
Be sure to put everything in(its)place.

Look for these indefinite pronouns (you can use your computer's search/find
function). If you find one, look to see if a pronoun refers to it. If so, be sure that
the pronoun is singular. Do not rely on the sound of the sentence; the plural pronoun may sound fine since it is often used in informal spoken English.

Not all indefinite pronouns are singular. *Both, many* and *few* are always plural.

Many of my friends have changed(their)majors.

These indefinite pronouns can be either singular or plural, depending on the
meaning of the sentence: *all, any, more, most, some.*

Some of the DVDs are missing from(their)shelf in the den.
Some of the essay strays from(its)thesis.

✳ CIRCLE *WHO* AND *WHOM* AND UNDERLINE THE REST OF THE CLAUSE

To choose the correct pronoun, circle *who* or *whom* and underline the rest of the **clause** (the word group with a subject and a verb). If the circled word acts as a subject, use *who*. If it is the object, use *whom*. Here are some examples:

> Hippocrates, (who or whom?) lived about 400 B.C., is called the "Father of Medicine."

Choose *who* because it is the subject of the verb *lived*.

> Hippocrates, who lived about 400 B.C., is called the "Father of Medicine."

> I attended the lecture by the Holocaust survivor (who or whom?) the community invited to speak.

Choose *whom* because it is the object of the verb *invited*.

> I attended the lecture by the Holocaust survivor whom the community invited to speak.

✳ SUBSTITUTE *HE* AND *HIM* FOR *WHO* AND *WHOM*

Often you can decide whether to use *who* or *whom* with this test: Use *who* where you could use *he*, and use *whom* where you could use *him*.

> I met the actor (who or whom?) starred in the long-running play.

We say, "*He* starred in the long-running play," so the correct form is *who*: I met the actor *who* starred in the long-running play.

> (Who or whom?) are you driving with?

We say, "You are driving with *him*," so the correct form is *whom*: Whom are you driving with?

✳ DETERMINE THE WORD *YOU* REFERS TO

You addresses the reader. If it refers to someone other than the reader, the result is a problem called **person shift.** To avoid this problem, mentally draw an arrow from *you* to the word it refers to. If this word names someone other than the reader, replace it with the correct pronoun. In this sentence, *you* refers to someone other than the reader:

> Distance runners must train religiously. (You) cannot compete successfully if (you) run only on weekends.

Here is the corrected version:

> Distance runners must train religiously. (They) cannot compete successfully if (they) run only on weekends.

If you compose at the computer, you can use its search/find function to locate and check each *you* in your draft.

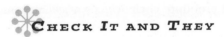

CHECK IT AND THEY

Check every *it* and *they* to be sure you have supplied a noun for each of these words to refer to. Otherwise, you will have a problem called **unstated reference.**

Unstated reference	Charlie is a very curious child. Because of <u>it</u>, he asks questions all the time.
Explanation	*It* cannot refer to *curious* because *curious* is a modifier, not a noun. The reference is meant to be *curiosity,* but that word is not stated.
Correction	Charlie is a very curious child. Because of his curiosity, he asks questions all the time.
Unstated reference	When I went to the unemployment office, <u>they</u> told me that some construction jobs were available.
Explanation	There is no stated noun for *they* to refer to.
Correction	When I went to the unemployment office, the employment counselor told me that some construction jobs were available.

AVOID UNCLEAR REFERENCE

When a pronoun can refer to more than one noun, the reader cannot tell what the writer means, creating a problem called **unclear reference.**

Unclear reference	Dad was in the garage with Brian when he heard the telephone ring.
Explanation	Because of unclear reference, the reader can't tell whether Dad or Brian heard the phone.
Correction	Dad was in the garage with Brian when Brian heard the telephone ring.

BE CAREFUL OF THIS AND WHICH

To avoid confusion, make sure that *this* and *which* refer to specific nouns.

Confusing	When people send e-mail, they expect an immediate response, whereas when they send a letter, they do not expect a quick reply. <u>This</u> interests communications specialists. (What interests communication specialists: people expecting an immediate response, people not expecting a quick reply, or the difference in expectations?)

Better   When people send e-mail, they expect an immediate response, whereas when they send a letter, they do not expect a quick reply. <u>This difference</u> interests communications specialists.

You can use your computer's search/find function to locate each *this* and *which* in your draft, so you can check your usage.

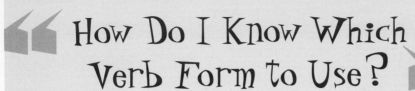

CHAPTER TWENTY-ONE

How Do I Know Which Verb Form to Use?

Choosing the right verb can be tricky at times, but the good news is that most of the problems arise in just a few special instances. Strategies for dealing with these instances are discussed in this chapter.

✳ CROSS OUT PHRASES BEFORE THE VERB

A phrase before the verb can trick you into choosing the wrong verb form. For example, which is correct?

The stack of books <u>is</u> about to fall.

The stack of books <u>are</u> about to fall.

To decide, cross out the phrase *of books,* and you can tell that the correct verb is *is.*

The stack ~~of books~~ is about to fall.

Phrases before the verb often begin with one of these words (called **prepositions**):

about	before	inside	over
above	between	into	through
across	by	like	to
after	during	near	toward
among	for	next	under
around	from	of	up
at	in	on	with

When in doubt about the correct verb form, cross out phrases beginning with one of these words. Here are some examples:

The container of old dishes (<u>is</u> or <u>are</u>?) on the landing.

The container ~~of old dishes~~ (<u>is</u> or <u>are</u>?) on the landing.

The container of old dishes <u>is</u> on the landing.

The herd of steers (<u>graze</u> or <u>grazes</u>?) contentedly.

The herd ~~of steers~~ (<u>graze</u> or <u>grazes</u>?) contentedly.

The herd of steers <u>grazes</u> contentedly.

The characteristics of the German shepherd (<u>make</u> or <u>makes</u>?) him a suitable show dog.

The characteristics ~~of the German shepherd~~ (<u>make</u> or <u>makes</u>?) him a suitable show dog.

The characteristics of the German shepherd <u>make</u> him a suitable show dog.

❄ REWRITE QUESTIONS

In sentences that ask questions, the verb comes before the subject. Verb choice is easier if you rewrite the sentence so it is no longer a question.

Sentence with question	(<u>Have</u> or <u>has</u>?) the students finished taking exams?
Sentence rewritten	The students <u>have</u> finished taking exams.
Sentence with question and correct verb	<u>Have</u> the students finished taking exams?

❄ REWRITE SENTENCES BEGINNING WITH *HERE* AND *THERE*

When a sentence begins with *here* or *there,* the verb comes before the subject. Rewrite the sentence putting the subject before the verb. The correct choice should be more apparent.

Sentence with *here*	Here (<u>is</u> or <u>are</u>?) the important papers you asked for.
Sentence rewritten	The important papers you asked for <u>are</u> here.
Sentence with *here* and correct verb	Here <u>are</u> the important papers you asked for.
Sentence with *there*	There (<u>was</u> or <u>were</u>?) an excellent dance band playing at the wedding reception.
Sentence rewritten	An excellent dance band <u>was</u> playing at the wedding reception.
Sentence with *there* and correct verb	There <u>was</u> an excellent dance band playing at the wedding reception.

❄ WATCH OUT FOR SUBJECTS JOINED BY *OR* AND *EITHER/OR*

Whether subjects joined by *or* and *either/or* (called **compound subjects**) take a singular or plural verb depends on what subjects are joined.

1. **If both subjects are singular, use a singular verb.**

   (Joyce) or (Rico) expects to pick me up for the concert.

   Either the (steak) or the (veal roast) is on sale at the market.

2. **If both subjects are plural, use a plural verb.**

   The (boxes) or the (fishing poles) are behind the door.

   Either the (scouts) or their (leaders) visit the elderly every week.

3. **If one subject is singular and the other is plural, place the plural subject second and use a plural verb.**

   The (gardenia) or the (roses) make a lovely centerpiece.

   Either my (sister) or my (brothers) cook Thanksgiving dinner each year.

WATCH OUT FOR INDEFINITE PRONOUNS

In formal usage, the **indefinite pronouns** *each, either, neither, one, none, no one, nothing, nobody, anyone, anybody, anything, everyone, everybody, everything, someone, somebody,* and *something* take singular verbs—even though the sense of the sentence suggests that a plural verb is logical. When you have used one of these words as the subject of a sentence, mentally circle the word and draw an arrow to the verb. Then check that verb to be sure it is singular.

(Each) of the students wants (not want) to have the test on Friday so the weekend is more relaxing.

(One) of the first museums was (not were) Altes Museum in Berlin.

(Either) of these vacation plans meets (not meet) your needs.

(Neither) of these paintings suits (not suit) my taste.

(None) of Lin's excuses is (not are) believable.

Do not rely on the sound of the sentence. The plural verb may sound fine, and the singular verb may sound a little off because the plural verb is often used in informal speech and writing. Nonetheless, use the singular verb for strict grammatical correctness in formal usage.

If you compose at the computer, you can use your search/find function to locate and check indefinite pronouns.

UNDERSTAND VERB TENSES

Tense means "time." Different verb tenses indicate different times.

1. Use the **present tense** to show the following:

Something is happening now   The committee members are meeting in room 2.

Something happens regularly Each year, the summer hurricane season <u>worries</u> coastal residents.

Something is true indefinitely She applied to Ohio State University, which <u>is</u> in Columbus, Ohio.

   2. Use the **past tense** to show that something took place before now:

The television series <u>was canceled</u> after two episodes.

Cass <u>left</u> for the store before I <u>arrived</u>.

   3. Use the **future tense** to show that something has not happened yet, but it will.

Next fall, the downtown reconstruction <u>will begin</u>.

   4. Use the **present perfect tense** to show the following:

Something began in the past and Already you <u>have painted</u> half of the kitchen.
continues into the present

Something began in the past Jake <u>has</u> finally <u>finished</u> the test.
and recently ended

Something happened at an I <u>have visited</u> Spain twice.
unspecified time in the past

   5. Use the **past perfect tense** to show that something happened in the past before something else happened in the past:

Dimitri said that Sophia <u>had left</u> before I arrived.

   6. Use the **future perfect tense** to indicate that one future event will occur before another future event.

By the end of the year, I <u>will have completed</u> a psychology minor.

   TIP: If you are unsure how to form the various verb tenses, consult a grammar handbook.

✳ LISTEN TO YOUR VERB TENSES

Tense means time. Many verbs change their form to show different tenses (times):

Present tense (time) Today I <u>walk</u> two miles for exercise.

Past tense (time) Yesterday I <u>walked</u> two miles for exercise.

Future tense (time) Tomorrow I <u>will walk</u> two miles for exercise.

   Sometimes a change in verb tense is necessary to show a change in time, but if you change tense inappropriately, you create a problem called **tense shift.**

Appropriate change in tense from present to past	I <u>recall</u> that April Fools' Day <u>began</u> in France.
Problem tense shift from present to past	After I <u>finish</u> my work, I <u>watched</u> a movie.

Read your draft out loud and listen to your verb tenses. If there are problem tense shifts, you are likely to hear them.

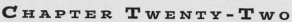

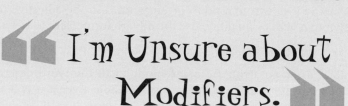

CHAPTER TWENTY-TWO

"I'm Unsure about Modifiers."

A modifier is a word or phrase that describes. Consider this sentence:

> Because of the serious accident, traffic moved slowly.

Because *serious* describes *accident, serious* is a modifier; because *slowly* describes *moved, slowly* is a modifier. Modifiers take different forms in different grammatical settings. If those forms give you some trouble, the suggestions in this chapter can help.

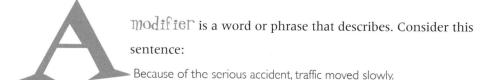

KNOW WHEN TO USE AN ADJECTIVE AND WHEN TO USE AN ADVERB

Which sentence is correct?

> The party ended so <u>abruptly</u> that no one had a chance to eat.
>
> The party ended so <u>abrupt</u> that no one had a chance to eat.

If you are unsure, you may have trouble knowing when to use adjectives and when to use adverbs. An **adjective** describes a noun or pronoun, and an **adverb** describes a verb or other modifier. Frequently, the adverb form ends in *-ly* and the adjective form does not.

Adjectives	Adverbs
brief	briefly
clear	clearly
loud	loudly
swift	swiftly

When in doubt, mentally draw an arrow from the modifier to the word it describes. If the arrow is drawn to a noun or pronoun, use the adjective form. If the arrow is drawn to a verb or modifier, use the adverb form. Here is an example:

Diane mowed the lawn (quick or quickly?) so she could leave with her friends.

To decide, mentally draw an arrow from the modifier to the word described. If the word described is a noun or a pronoun, use the adjective; if it is a verb or another modifier, use the adverb (which often ends in *-ly*).

Diane mowed the lawn (quick or quickly?) so she could leave with her friends.

Now you can tell that *quickly* is called for because a verb is described:

Diane mowed the lawn quickly so she could leave with her friends.

Here are some more examples:

David was (absolute or absolutely?) sure of the answer.

David was absolutely sure of the answer. (A modifier is described, so the adverb is used.)

The ancient Egyptians thought of the soul as a bird that could fly around (easy or easily?).

The ancient Egyptians thought of the soul as a bird that could fly around easily. (A verb is described, so the adverb is used.)

Chris is (happy or happily?) that he was promoted after only one month on the job.

Chris is happy that he was promoted after only one month on the job. (A noun is described, so the adjective is used.)

❋ REMEMBER THAT *GOOD* IS AN ADJECTIVE AND *WELL* IS AN ADVERB—WITH ONE CAUTION AND ONE EXCEPTION

Good is an adjective; it describes nouns and pronouns:

The good news is that I got the job.

Well is an adverb; it describes verbs and modifiers:

After 10 years of lessons, Maxine plays the piano well.

Now here's the caution: After verbs like *taste, seem, appear,* and *look,* use *good* because the noun or pronoun before the verb is being described.

The meat tastes good, even though it is overcooked.

Claudia looks good, although she just had surgery.

The restaurant seems good, so let's eat here.

And here's the exception: *Well* is used as an adjective to mean "in good health."

After six brownies and a bottle of soda, the child did not feel well.

If you compose at the computer, use the search/find function to locate each *good* and *well* in your draft, so you can check your usage.

❋ Do Not Use More or Most with an *-er* or *-est* Form

Yes: I like tacos <u>better</u> than nachos.

No: I like tacos <u>more better</u> than nachos.

Yes: The Sahara Desert is the world's <u>hottest</u> region in summer.

No: The Sahara Desert is the world's <u>most hottest</u> region in summer.

Yes: The Sahara Desert is <u>bigger</u> than the United States.

No: The Sahara Desert is <u>more bigger</u> than the United States.

Yes: The <u>rainiest</u> place on Earth is Mount Waialeale in Hawaii.

No: The <u>most rainiest</u> place on Earth is Mount Waialeale in Hawaii.

❋ Check Sentences That Open with *-ing* or *-ed* Verb Forms

An *-ing* or *-ed* verb form (called a **participle**) can be used as an adjective:

Whistling, Carolyn strolled through the park.

Whistling is a verb form that is used as an adjective to describe *Carolyn*.

Living only two or three years, lizards have a short life span.

Living is a verb form used as an adjective to describe *lizards*.

When an *-ing* or *-ed* form opens a sentence, it must be followed by the subject that the form describes. Otherwise, the result will be a **dangling modifier.** Dangling modifiers can create silly sentences:

Dangling modifier	While making the coffee, the toast burned. (This sentence says that the toast made the coffee.)
Correction	While making the coffee, I burned the toast. (The opening *-ing* verb form is followed by a subject it can sensibly describe.)
Dangling modifier	Exhausted from work, a nap was needed. (This sentence says that the nap was exhausted.)
Correction	Exhausted from work, Lucy needed a nap. (The opening *-ed* verb form is followed by a subject it can sensibly describe.)

If you are in the habit of writing dangling modifiers, check every opening *-ing* and *-ed* verb form to be sure it is closely followed by a subject it can sensibly describe.

✳ PLACE MODIFIERS NEAR THE WORDS THEY DESCRIBE

If a modifier is too far from the word it describes, the result is a **misplaced modifier.** A misplaced modifier can create a silly sentence:

Misplaced modifier Lee bought a bicycle from a neighbor with a flat tire. (The sentence says that the neighbor had a flat tire.)

Correction Lee bought a bicycle with a flat tire from a neighbor. (The modifier has been moved closer to the word it describes.)

CHAPTER TWENTY-THREE

" Can't I Just Place a Comma Wherever I Pause? "

Placing commas wherever you pause is a gamble: Sometimes the gamble pays off, and sometimes it doesn't. Your better bet is to learn the rules. Editing strategies in this chapter will help you follow these common comma rules:

1. Use a comma after an introductory element.
2. Use a comma before a coordinating conjunction that joins independent clauses.
3. Use a comma to separate items in a series.
4. Use a comma to set off nonessential sentence elements.

For other important comma rules, consult a grammar handbook.

FIND THE SUBJECT AND LOOK IN FRONT OF IT

Anything that comes before the subject of a sentence is an **introductory element** and should be set off with a comma. It does not matter whether the material is one word, a phrase, or a clause. Thus, once you identify the subject of a sentence, you can look in front of it. If there are any words there, follow them with a comma, like this:

Word before the subject	Surprisingly, the heart of a whale beats only nine times a minute.
Phrase before the subject	In medieval Japan, fashionable women blackened their teeth to enhance their appearance.
Clause before the subject	Although Albert Einstein developed the theory of relativity, he failed his first college entrance exam.

✳ FIND THE COORDINATING CONJUNCTIONS, AND THEN LOOK LEFT AND RIGHT

The following words are **coordinating conjunctions;** you can remember them by remembering *fanboys,* the word formed by the first letter of each word:

for   and   nor   but   or   yet   so

If a coordinating conjunction joins two word groups that can stand as sentences **(independent clauses),** place a comma before the conjunction.

To apply this rule, mentally circle every coordinating conjunction; then look left and right. If an independent clause appears on both sides, place a comma before the conjunction.

Use comma
independent clause
[I enjoy reading Stephen King novels], (but) [I do not enjoy watching
independent clause
horror movies.]

Use comma
independent clause
[The Centers for Disease Control predicts a flu outbreak], (so) [I plan
independent clause
to get a flu shot.]

Use comma
independent clause   independent clause
[Fish can distinguish colors], (and) [they actually prefer some colors over others.]

Do not use comma
not a clause
The owl cannot move its eyes (but) [can turn its head around.]

Do not use comma
not a clause
The car accelerated quickly (and) [turned left.]

Do not use comma
not a clause
You can leave with me now (or) [wait until later.]

If you compose at the computer and you are unsure whether to use a comma before a coordinating conjunction, underline the words before and after the conjunction. Examine both sets of words. If they *both* could stand as sentences, use the comma. If neither one can be a sentence or if only one can be a sentence, do *not* use a comma.

✳ LOOK FOR SERIES

A **series** is three or more words, phrases, or clauses. Separate the items in a series with commas.

Words in a series   This restaurant specializes in <u>pasta</u>, <u>steak</u>, <u>salads</u>, and <u>seafood</u>.

Phrases in a series Recycling centers have been established <u>at the government center</u>, <u>behind the high school</u>, and <u>at the baseball fields</u>.

Clauses in a series <u>The manager lowered prices</u>, <u>the sales staff tried to be more helpful</u>, and <u>the owner remodeled the store</u>.

IDENTIFY NONESSENTIAL ELEMENTS

A **nonessential element** can be removed without changing the meaning of the sentence. Identify nonessential elements and set them off with commas. In the following sentences, the nonessential elements are underlined as a study aid.

Nonessential word	The president at the time, <u>Clinton</u>, worked to achieve the Egyptian–Israeli peace agreement.
Nonessential word	The governor, <u>surprisingly</u>, opposed the balanced-budget amendment.
Nonessential phrase	You can, <u>of course</u>, join us for dinner.
Nonessential phrase	The crime rate, <u>according to the newspaper</u>, has not increased this year.
Nonessential clause	Very few people understand how the election process works, <u>if you ask me</u>.
Nonessential clause	Amy Winehouse, <u>who died of a drug overdose</u>, was a talented performer.

If you compose at the computer and are unsure whether an element is nonessential, delete the element and see if necessary meaning is lost. If necessary meaning is *not* lost, use commas. After deciding, put the deleted element back in the sentence. For example, in the following sentence, is the underlined element nonessential?

Sergeant Shepherd <u>who was awarded a Purple Heart</u> is reenlisting.

Use the delete key to get

Sergeant Shepherd is reenlisting.

Because necessary meaning is not lost (we can still tell who is reenlisting), the element is nonessential. Therefore, use commas.

Sergeant Shepherd, who was awarded a Purple Heart, is reenlisting.

Here is another sentence. Is the underlined element nonessential?

The sergeant <u>who was awarded a Purple Heart</u> is reenlisting.

Use the delete key to get

The sergeant is reenlisting.

Necessary meaning is lost because we cannot tell which sergeant is reenlisting. Therefore, the element is essential, and commas are not used.

The sergeant who was awarded a Purple Heart is reenlisting.

CHAPTER TWENTY-FOUR

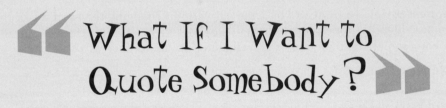

"What If I Want to Quote Somebody?"

Sometimes, you want to use the words someone has spoken or written, perhaps to advance a story, add vividness, lend insight into character, or support an idea. When you quote someone, you are obligated to get it right. That means you must reproduce the words *exactly* as they were spoken or written, and it means you must follow the punctuation and capitalization rules in this chapter.

CONSIDER WHERE IN THE SENTENCE THE QUOTATION OCCURS

If your quotation comes *after* the statement of who spoke, model this form:

> Eli reminded us, "Remember to put out the campfire before retiring."

If your quotation comes *before* the statement of who spoke, model this form:

> "Remember to put out the campfire before retiring," Eli reminded us.

If your quotation comes both before and after the statement of who spoke, model the first form if the first part does *not* form a sentence. Model the second form if it does.

> "Remember," Eli reminded us, "to put out the campfire before retiring."

> "Remember to put out the campfire before retiring," Eli reminded us. "You don't want to start a forest fire."

DETERMINE WHETHER THE QUOTATION OR THE ENTIRE SENTENCE ASKS A QUESTION

When the quotation asks a question, model one of these forms:

The reporter asked Senator McEwin, "Did you vote for the trade bill?"

"Did you vote for the trade bill?" the reporter asked Senator McEwin.

When the entire sentence asks a question, model this form:

Did the newspaper really say, "The president of the school board plans to resign"?

(The question mark appears outside the quotation mark.)

REPRODUCE A PERSON'S THOUGHTS AS A QUOTATION

Treat a person's thoughts like spoken words.

Julia thought, "It's time I made a change in my life."

BE SURE YOU REALLY HAVE EXACT WORDS

Before using quotation marks, be sure you are reproducing someone's exact words.

Use quotation marks (exact words)	The police officer said, "Move your car."
Do not use quotation marks (not exact words)	The police officer said that you should move your car.

PLAGIARISM ALERT

You will be guilty of plagiarism if you pass off someone else's words as your own. Therefore, each time you use the exact words of another person, be sure to enclose those words in quotation marks, according to the conventions explained in this chapter. In addition, you cannot alter the spoken or written words, for that, too, is plagiarism.

A convenience of using the Internet is the ability to copy and paste material from websites. However, *any* material you copy must appear in quotation marks and must be acknowledged according to the conventions explained in Chapter 29.

CHAPTER TWENTY-FIVE

"I Have Trouble with Apostrophes."

Apostrophes have two main functions: They take the place of missing letters in contractions, and they signal possession. Some people think apostrophes have a third function: to drive them crazy. Apostrophes *can* be pesky, so if you are unsure how to use them, try the techniques in this chapter.

IDENTIFY THE MISSING LETTER(S) IN A CONTRACTION

A **contraction** is formed by taking two words, dropping one or more letters, and joining the two words into one. An apostrophe is placed at the site of the missing letter(s). For example, the contraction form of *did not* is *didn't*. Because the *o* is left out of *not*, the apostrophe is placed between the *n* and the *t*. Here are some more examples:

have + not = haven't (apostrophe at site of missing *o*)

we + will = we'll (apostrophe at site of missing *wi*)

it + is = it's (apostrophe at site of missing *i*)

NOTE: The contraction form of *will not* is the unusual *won't*.

USE IT'S ONLY WHEN YOU CAN SUBSTITUTE "IT IS" OR "IT HAS"

1. *It's* is the contraction form of *it is* or *it has*.

It's time for a change of leadership in this state.

(It is time for a change of leadership in this state.)

It's been 10 years since I smoked a cigarette.

(It has been 10 years since I smoked a cigarette.)

2. *Its* is a possessive form; it shows ownership and cannot be substituted for *it is* or *it has*.

Yes: The river overflowed its banks. (*Its* shows ownership.)

No: The river overflowed it's banks.

Yes: It's too late to turn back now. (*It's* here means *it is*.)

No: Its too late to turn back now.

Avoid Contractions

No law says that you *must* use contractions. If you are unsure where to place the apostrophe, use the two-word form instead of the contraction.

Use the "Of" Test

If you can add a phrase beginning with *of* to a noun or indefinite pronoun and reword, the noun or indefinite pronoun is possessive and needs an apostrophe to show that possession.

Is an apostrophe needed?	The books pages are beginning to curl.
Add an *of* phrase	The pages of the book are beginning to curl.
Apostrophe is needed	The book's pages are beginning to curl.
Is an apostrophe needed?	Someones car is parked in a no parking zone.
Add an *of* phrase	The car of someone is parked in a no parking zone.
Apostrophe is needed	Someone's car is parked in a no parking zone.
Is an apostrophe needed?	The steak knives on the counter are very sharp.
Add an *of* phrase	The knives of steak on the counter are very sharp.
No apostrophe is needed	The steak knives on the counter are very sharp.

For Possessive Forms, Ask Two Questions

Apostrophes are used with nouns to show possession. To determine how to use the apostrophe, ask, "Does the noun end in *s?*"

1. If the noun *does not* end in *s,* add an apostrophe and an *s,* like this:

President + 's = President's

The President's Council on Aging reports an increase in homelessness among the elderly.

children + 's = children's

Children's toys cost more money than they are worth.

2. If the noun *does* end in *s*, ask, "Is the noun singular or plural?"

   a. If the noun is singular, add an apostrophe and an *s*, like this:

      Delores + 's = Delores's

      Delores's new car was hit in the parking lot.

      bus + 's = bus's

      The bus's brakes jammed, causing a minor accident.

   b. If the noun is plural, add an apostrophe, like this:

      shoes + ' = shoes'

      All the shoes' laces are too long.

      mayors + ' = mayors'

      The three mayors' mutual aid agreement will yield economic benefits.

❋ WATCH OUT FOR NOUN PLURALS

Simple noun plurals do *not* include apostrophes because they do not show possession.

Yes: The most valuable player pitched three <u>no-hitters</u> this year.

No: The most valuable player pitched three <u>no-hitter's</u> this year.

Yes: Three tropical <u>storms</u> are currently churning in the Atlantic Ocean.

No: Three tropical <u>storms'</u> are currently churning in the Atlantic Ocean.

❋ WATCH OUT FOR POSSESSIVE PRONOUNS

These words are **possessive pronouns** because they show ownership: *his, her, hers, your, yours, their, theirs, our, ours,* and *its.* Since these words are already possessive, do not use them with apostrophes. (Remember that *its* is the possessive pronoun, and *it's* is the contraction form of *it is* and *it has.*)

Yes: <u>His</u> backpack was left in the car.

No: <u>His'</u> backpack was left in the car.

Yes: Are the sneakers under the couch <u>yours</u>?

No: Are the sneakers under the couch <u>your's</u>?

Check Each Noun Ending in *s*

If you tend to forget apostrophes for possessives, check each noun ending in *s*. If any of those nouns shows ownership, be sure to place an apostrophe.

Use Your Computer's Spell Check Cautiously

Computer spell check programs are very helpful, but many do not check apostrophes in contractions, so misspellings such as *cant* may not be flagged. Further, most spell checks do not distinguish between *its* and *it's*.

CHAPTER TWENTY-SIX

"I Never Know What to Capitalize."

Ask people how they know what to capitalize, and many will say they aren't sure, so they just capitalize "the important stuff." Are you one of those people? If so, how do you know what's "important"? This chapter can help you use capital letters with more confidence.

CAPITALIZE THE NAMES OF ANIMALS AND PEOPLE AND THE TITLES BEFORE PEOPLE'S NAMES

Capitalize   John, Lassie, Seabiscuit, Aunt Rhoda, Professor DeMatteo, Rabbi Gold
Do not capitalize   boy, dog, horse, my aunt, a professor, the rabbi

NOTE: Always capitalize the pronoun *I*.

CAPITALIZE TITLES OF RELATIVES SUBSTITUTED FOR NAMES

Capitalize   I bought <u>Mother and Dad</u> a Blu-ray player for their anniversary.
Do not capitalize   I bought <u>my mother and dad</u> a Blu-ray player for their anniversary.

CAPITALIZE SPECIFIC GEOGRAPHIC LOCATIONS, NAMES OF NATIONALITIES, AND ADJECTIVES DERIVED FROM THEM

Capitalize   Africa, Grand Canyon, Baltic Sea, Atlanta, Georgia, Mahoning Avenue, Stark County, Route 82, the Middle East, the Pacific Northwest, the West Coast, Chinese cooking, Irish linen

Do not capitalize   continent, a canyon, sea, city, one state, the avenue, county, the northwestern region, the western part of the country

✳ CAPITALIZE RELIGIONS, SACRED BOOKS, AND WORDS AND PRONOUNS THAT REFER TO GOD

Capitalize   God, the Lord, Allah, the Torah, the New Testament, Muslim, Catholicism, the Holy Bible, the Trinity, Jewish, in His wisdom, God is just

Do not capitalize   the gods, a deity, a sacred text

✳ CAPITALIZE SPECIFIC DAYS, MONTHS, AND HOLIDAYS

Capitalize   Monday, June, Halloween

Do not capitalize   day, month, holiday, winter

✳ CAPITALIZE SPECIFIC BRAND NAMES

Capitalize   Mountain Dew, Pillsbury cake mix, Reebok tennis shoes, Cheerios, Buick

Do not capitalize   soda pop, cake mix, tennis shoes, cereal, car

✳ CAPITALIZE SPECIFIC ORGANIZATIONS, COMPANIES, AND BUILDINGS

Capitalize   General Motors, Walt Disney World, Indiana University, the Empire State Building, the Fraternal Order of Police, the Red Cross

Do not capitalize   car manufacturer, amusement park, college, building, fraternity, club, company

✳ CAPITALIZE SPECIFIC HISTORIC EVENTS, DOCUMENTS, AND PERIODS

Capitalize   the Constitution of the United States, the Battle of the Bulge, Korean War, the Magna Carta, the Renaissance

Do not capitalize   a country's constitution, a battle, the war, document, historical period

CAPITALIZE TITLES CORRECTLY

Capitalize the first and last words of a title and a subtitle, no matter what those words are. In between, capitalize everything except articles *(a, an, the)*, short conjunctions (such as *and, but, or, nor, for, so, yet, since*), and short prepositions (such *as in, on, at, of, by*).

In the Heat of the Night   *Pirates of the Caribbean: The Curse of the Black Pearl*

The Catcher in the Rye   *Making Peace with Your Past: How to Be Happy*

USE YOUR COMPUTER'S TOOLS

Your word processing program may allow you to correct automatically words you routinely capitalize incorrectly (such as *civil war* instead of *Civil War*). Be sure to learn how to use that feature.

Use your computer's spell check, but know that it is more likely to identify words that you have *not* capitalized than words you have capitalized inappropriately.

CAPITALIZE E-MAIL CORRECTLY

In e-mail you write for school, work, or any formal and semiformal situations, follow the capitalization rules. Using all capitals is like electronic shouting; using all lowercase can be confusing.

CHAPTER TWENTY-SEVEN

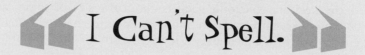

I Can't Spell.

First the bad news: Misspelled words can undermine your reader's confidence in your writing ability. Now the good news: You can solve spelling problems with the techniques in this chapter.

WHEN IN DOUBT, CHECK IT OUT

When it comes to using a dictionary, we all get lazy. Still, the only surefire way to check a spelling is to look up the word. If you have the slightest suspicion that a word is misspelled, check the dictionary.

BUY TWO DICTIONARIES

Buy two dictionaries: a hardback collegiate dictionary to keep on your writing desk and a paperback one to carry with you. You are more likely to look up a word if you have a dictionary at hand and do not have to get up and walk somewhere. Of course, if you compose at the computer, you can use an online dictionary, such as Dictionary.com.

USE A PRONUNCIATION DICTIONARY

If you have trouble finding words in a traditional dictionary, try using a pronunciation dictionary that lets you find words according to the way they sound.

USE A SPELLING DICTIONARY

Spelling dictionaries, available in most bookstores, reference frequently misspelled words. They provide spellings without definitions, so they are thin and convenient to carry around.

Use a Pocket Spell Checker

Pocket spell checkers are electronic gadgets about the size of some calculators. They can be expensive, but if you are more inclined to check spellings with an electronic gizmo than with a dictionary, they are worth the money.

Tape a List to Your Computer or Desk

Keep a list of the words you frequently misspell or misuse taped to your computer or desk for a ready reference.

Learn Correct Pronunciations

Sometimes people misspell because they pronounce a word incorrectly. For example, you may misspell *February* if you pronounce it "Feb · u · ary"; you may misspell *preventive* if you pronounce it "pre · ven · ta · tive."

Break a Word into Parts

When a word is composed of identifiable parts, spell the word out part by part, so it is more manageable.

under · stand · able	with · hold	arm · chair
room · mate	kinder · garten	dis · ease
comfort · able	lone · liness	over · coat

Break a Word into Syllables

Some words are more easily spelled if you go syllable by syllable.

or · gan · i · za · tion	cit · i · zen	mon · u · men · tal
Jan · u · ar · y	in · vi · ta · tion	hos · pi · tal
in · di · vis · i · ble	con · ver · sa · tion	pro · ba · bly

Look for Prefixes

When a **prefix** (word beginning) is added to a word, the spelling of the base word usually does not change.

mis · take	dis · satisfaction	mis · spell
un · nerve	un · necessary	pre · pare
mis · inform	inter · related	pre · record

Use Memory Tricks

Think of tricks to help you spell words. For example, the word *instrument* contains *strum,* and you strum a guitar, which is an instrument. Actors in a *tragedy* often *rage* at each other.

Memory tricks can be particularly helpful for pairs of words that are often mistaken for each other. You may like some of the following tricks, and you may want to make up tricks for other pairs of words that you confuse.

1. **advice/advise**

   a. *Advice* means "a suggestion."

      Joel's <u>advice</u> proved sound.

   b. *Advise* means "to give advice."

      Yvette is the best person to <u>advise</u> you.

MEMORY TRICK: A person with a <u>vice</u> needs ad<u>vice</u>.

2. **affect/effect**

   a. *Affect* means "to influence."

      The drought will <u>affect</u> the economy for years to come.

   b. *Effect* means "result."

      The <u>effects</u> of the drought are devastating.

MEMORY TRICK: The first syllable of <u>effect</u> rhymes with the first syllable of <u>result</u>.

3. **among/between**

   a. *Among* is used for more than two.

      Divide the candy <u>among</u> the four children.

   b. *Between* is used for two.

      The difference <u>between</u> the ages of Phil and Carlos is not important.

MEMORY TRICK: Can you fit anything <u>between</u> the <u>two e's</u> in the last syllable of <u>between</u>?

4. **beside/besides**

   a. *Beside* means "alongside of."

      I parked the van <u>beside</u> the Corvette.

   b. *Besides* means "in addition to."

      <u>Besides</u> good soil, the plants need water.

MEMORY TRICK: The final <u>s</u> in <u>besides</u> is "in addition to" the first <u>s</u>.

5. **fewer/less**

   a. *Fewer* is for things that can be counted.

     Fewer people voted in this election than in the last one.

   b. *Less* is used for things that cannot be counted.

     People who exercise regularly experience less stress than those who do not.

MEMORY TRICK: Think of countless. Less is used for things that cannot be counted.

6. **then/than**

   a. *Then* refers to a certain time.

     The trumpets blared; then the cymbals crashed.

   b. *Than* is used to compare.

     I like small classes better than large lectures.

MEMORY TRICK: Think of the e in then and time; think of the a in than and compare.

LEARN THE HOMOPHONES

Homophones sound alike, but they are spelled and used differently. Learn the following homophones and any others that give you trouble.

1. **all ready/already**

   a. *All ready* means "all set."

     By three o'clock, the family was all ready to leave for Virginia Beach.

   b. *Already* means "by this time."

     We are already an hour behind schedule, and we haven't begun the trip yet.

2. **bridal/bridle**

   a. *Bridal* pertains to brides.

     Lorraine and Gary's bridal party danced all night at the wedding reception.

   b. *Bridle* is part of a horse's head gear.

     The horse's bridle did not fit properly.

3. **buy/by**

   a. *Buy* is a verb meaning "purchase."

     With my refund check, I plan to buy a Blu-ray player.

   b. *By* is a preposition meaning "near" or "a means of."

     The best way to travel in New York City is by subway .

4. **capital/capitol**

   a. *Capital* is the seat of government or an uppercase letter.

   The <u>capital</u> of Ohio is spelled with a <u>capital</u> C.

   b. *Capitol* is a building. The word is capitalized when it refers to the building in Washington, D.C.

   The <u>Capitol</u> in Washington, D.C., is a popular tourist destination.

5. **flour/flower**

   a. *Flour* is the ingredient used in baking.

   Two cups of <u>flour</u> are required for this recipe.

   b. *Flower* is the plant that blooms.

   A single <u>flower</u> was placed on each table.

6. **hear/here**

   a. *Hear* means "listen."

   I can't <u>hear</u> you over the noise of the crowd.

   b. *Here* means "a nearby place."

   <u>Here</u> is where we should pitch the tent.

7. **its/it's**

   a. *Its* shows ownership.

   The car hit a pothole and broke <u>its</u> axle.

   b. *It's* is the contraction form of "it is" or "it has."

   <u>It's</u> too late to say you are sorry.

   <u>It's</u> been 10 years since graduation.

8. **knew/new**

   a. *Knew* is the past tense of *know*.

   If I <u>knew</u> you were coming, I would have cooked more food.

   b. *New* is the opposite of old.

   My <u>new</u> shoes are a half size too small.

9. **know/no**

   a. *Know* means "understand" or "have knowledge of."

   For the biology exam, the class must <u>know</u> the parts of a cell.

   b. *No* expresses a negative idea or the idea of zero.

   <u>No</u> person can say <u>no</u> to such a good idea.

10. **passed/past**

   a. *Passed* means "went by" or "handed."

   The shooting star <u>passed</u> overhead at nine o'clock.

   Katie <u>passed</u> the potatoes to Earvin.

   b. *Past* refers to previous time. It also means "by."

   I have learned from <u>past</u> experience not to trust Jerry.

   When I drove <u>past</u> the house, no one was home.

11. **principal/principle**

   a. *Principal* means "main" or "most important." It is also the school official.

   The <u>principal</u> roadblock to peace is the personalities of the country's leaders.

   The high school <u>principal</u> favors a dress code.

   b. *Principle* is a truth or standard.

   The <u>principles</u> of world economics are studied in this course.

12. **there/their/they're**

   a. *There* refers to direction or place. It also opens sentences.

   Place the vase of flowers <u>there</u> on the coffee table.

   <u>There</u> is a surprise for you in the kitchen.

   b. *Their* shows ownership.

   The students revised <u>their</u> drafts in the computer lab.

   c. *They're* is the contraction form of "they are."

   Do not sit Lee and Dana next to each other; <u>they're</u> not getting along.

13. **threw/through**

   a. *Threw* is the past tense of *throw*.

   The shortstop <u>threw</u> the ball to the pitcher.

   b. *Through* means "in one side and out the other" or "finished."

   I had trouble getting the thread <u>through</u> the needle.

   My morning biology class is not <u>through</u> until 11:00 o'clock.

14. **to/too/two**

   a. *To* means "toward." It is also used with a verb to form the **infinitive.**

   Liza usually walks <u>to</u> school.

   Eric is learning how <u>to</u> play the violin.

   b. *Too* means "excessively" or "also."

   I find it <u>too</u> hot in this building.

   Juanita works in the library, and she tutors math <u>too</u>.

  c. *Two* is the number.

   <u>Two</u> weeks ago, I bought a new car.

15. who's/whose

  a. *Who's* is the contraction form of "who is" or "who has."

   <u>Who's</u> the person standing with Mike?

  b. *Whose* shows ownership.

   Bilal is the boy <u>whose</u> poem won the award.

16. your/you're

  a. *Your* shows ownership.

   You left your keys in the car.

  b. *You're* is the contraction form of "you are."

   If <u>you're</u> leaving now, please take me with you.

UNDERLINE WORDS TO CHECK LATER

While drafting or revising, you may sense that a word is spelled wrong. Yet looking the word up at that point is inefficient because it interrupts the drafting or revising momentum. To solve this problem, underline every word whose spelling you are unsure of as you write it. Then you have a visual reminder to look up the word later, when it is more convenient.

KEEP A SPELLING LIST

Look up the words you misspell and add the words, correctly spelled, to a list for study. Each day, study the list and memorize another word or two in an effort to increase the number of words you can spell.

USE YOUR COMPUTER'S AUTOCORRECT FEATURE

Your word processing program may allow you to correct automatically words you routinely misspell (such as *defanite* instead of *definite*). Learn to use that feature.

USE YOUR COMPUTER'S SPELL CHECK CAUTIOUSLY

Spell checks test every word you have written against the words in the program's dictionary, and that dictionary will likely be smaller than a collegiate dictionary. If a word is not recognized, the spell check will offer alternative spellings. If the spell check comes across a typing error, it may be baffled if nothing in its memory comes close to the spelling. Also, homophones (soundalikes) are untouched by spell checks, so the confusion of something like *there, their, they're* will not be resolved. Finally, resist the temptation to accept automatically the first spelling offered by a spell check, as it may not be the one you should use. Despite these limitations, spell checks can be helpful to people with chronic spelling problems.

PART V

A Troubleshooting Guide to Research

You can conduct research to draw on the words and ideas of other writers. For example, when you write a long research paper, you use multiple sources to examine a topic in depth. Such a paper may include more source material than your own ideas. You can also use sources in a shorter essay by including the words and ideas of other writers to support your own ideas. In this case, the writing will be mostly your ideas, supplemented by source material.

Whether you are using sources in a research paper or in a shorter paper that is largely your own ideas, you must use those sources *responsibly*. This section of the book will show you how.

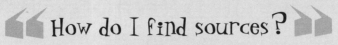

TROUBLESHOOTING STRATEGIES

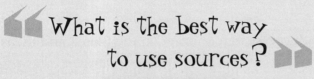

How do I find sources?

Have you tried these?

❑ Taking a library tour **(p. 153)**   ❑ Using indexes **(p. 155)**

What is the best way to use sources?

Have you tried these?

❑ Paraphrasing **(p. 159)**   ❑ Quoting **(p. 160)**

CHAPTER TWENTY-EIGHT

"How Do I Find Good Sources—and Why Do I Need Them?"

As a writer, you don't have to "know it all"—you can explain or prove your points with help from other writers by using sources. Here are some examples:

- In an essay arguing that juveniles who commit murder should not be tried in court as adults, you can quote a judge who says that adult courts are not set up to protect the rights of juveniles.

- In an essay explaining the benefits of a high-protein diet, you can give the view of a nutritionist who believes that high-protein diets are healthful.

- In an essay explaining how Internet predators work, you can summarize a newspaper account of how one such predator met children online.

- In an essay calling for an end to teacher tenure, you can give background information by looking up and explaining how, when, and why tenure became a part of American education.

This chapter will help you locate suitable sources in the library and on the Internet to use in your writing.

GET TO KNOW YOUR CAMPUS LIBRARY

Many campus libraries offer self-guided tours, tours conducted by librarians, or workshops to familiarize students with the library. Take a tour or participate in a workshop, so you are aware of your library's resources and how to use them efficiently.

❋ CONSIDER YOUR NEEDS

To save time and energy in the library and online, know what you're looking for. Perhaps you need a statistic to back up your observation that academic cheating is on the rise, or perhaps you want a quotation from a psychologist who believes that violent video games do not harm adolescent males. Maybe you want historical background on the nation's affirmative action laws. Knowing what you need keeps you focused.

❋ CONSULT YOUR CAMPUS REFERENCE LIBRARIAN

The reference librarian in your school's library (sometimes called the media center) is a trained researcher who can help you find print and electronic resources. This person can both save you time and teach you valuable search strategies, so you can function more independently in the future.

❋ USE REFERENCE WORKS

Located in the reference section, reference works include general encyclopedias, subject encyclopedias, almanacs, dictionaries, biographical dictionaries, and yearbooks. These works, which can be in paper form, on CD-ROM, or on the Internet, are excellent for locating specific information, such as facts, statistics, and dates. Particularly helpful are the following:

- General subject encyclopedias such as *Encyclopedia Britannica* provide an overview of a broad range of subjects.
- Subject encyclopedias such as *Encyclopedia of Education, Encyclopedia of Feminism,* and *Encyclopedia of Film and Television* provide more in-depth information on specific subjects.
- Almanacs and yearbooks such as *The World Almanac, Information Please Almanac,* and *Facts on File* provide statistics and information on current events.
- *Statistical Abstract of the United States* provides information on population and American institutions.
- The *Congressional Record* provides information about what has occurred in Congress.
- Biographical dictionaries such as *Current Biography* and *Webster's New Biographical Dictionary* provide information on people.

For the titles of other useful reference works, speak to a librarian.

Use the Computerized Catalog to Locate Books

The reference section of your library provides a computer catalog of every book in the library. In many cases, you can also access the catalog from your own computer or sites around campus. Easy-to-follow directions should be posted near the library computers. Follow them to type in your writing topic, and books on that topic will be listed on the screen. If any of those books look helpful, write down the call numbers and use those numbers to find the books.

If you do not find books on your topic, you may be using the wrong search term. Look up your topic in the *Library of Congress Subject Headings* book, usually located near the computer catalog terminals. You will find the search term you should use as the keyword(s) in your subject search at the computer catalog.

Use Indexes to Locate Magazine, Journal, and Newspaper Articles

Magazines, journals, and newspaper articles often have the most current information. To find useful articles, look up your topic in a print, online, or CD-ROM index located in the reference room. The following indexes are a good starting point:

- *Academic Search Premier*
- *Applied Science and Technology Index*
- *Art Index*
- *Business Periodicals Index*
- *Current Index to Journals in Education*
- *EBSCO Host*
- *Film Index*
- *General Science Index*
- *Government Publications Index*
- *Humanities Index*
- *Infotrac*
- *Lexis-Nexis*
- *Music Index*
- *New York Times Index*
- *Proquest*
- *Reader's Guide to Periodical Literature*
- *Resources in Education*
- *Science Source*
- *Social Sciences Index*
- *Sociological Abstracts*
- *Women: A Bibliography*

Use Abstracts and Bibliographies to Locate Books and Journal Articles on Specific Subjects

An **abstract** lists journal articles by subject matter and gives a brief summary of each article's content. A **bibliography** lists both books and journal articles. Here is a list of some helpful abstracts and bibliographies that may be available in your campus library in print, on CD-ROM, or online:

- *Bibliography of Modern History*
- *Bibliography on Women*
- *Biological Abstracts*
- *Chemical Abstracts*
- *Drama Bibliography*
- *ERIC* (education)
- *Historical Abstracts*
- *International Bibliography of Geography*
- *MLA Bibliography* (language and literature)

Search the Internet

If your topic is very current or of local scope, your best bet for useful sources may be online. Type your topic into a **search engine,** which is a program that locates websites and web pages on whatever topic you enter into the "search" box. You may find the following search engines helpful:

www.altavista.com
www.dogpile.com
www.excite.com
www.google.com
www.metacrawler.com
www.yahoo.com

For a guide to helpful Internet search tools, visit this site:

http://itools.com/information

Use Online References

The following reference tools, which are available online, can lead you to useful information available on the Internet:

Biography.com:	www.biography.com
Internet Public Library:	www.ipl.org

Library Spot:	www.libraryspot.com
Online Newspapers:	www.onlinenewspapers.com
Online Newspapers and Magazines:	www.metagrid.com
Reference Desk:	www.refdesk.com
Information Please:	www.infoplease.com
World Wide Web Virtual LIbrary:	www.vlib.org

USE HIGH-QUALITY SOURCES

Evaluate each of your sources for reliability and quality. These guidelines can help:

- Be sure the source is recent enough. If your topic is General Sherman's march through Georgia during the Civil War, a source from 1967 may be fine. However, if you are researching AIDS vaccines, a 2000 source is outdated.

- Determine whether the author has a particular bias or political leaning. A website sponsored by the National Rifle Association may not give you a balanced view of the gun control issue, and a site sponsored by Planned Parenthood may not give you a balanced view of abortion.

- Check the author's credentials. Look at book jackets, websites, and headnotes to learn about the author's publications, education, current position, and affiliations. If necessary, look up the author in a biographical dictionary.

- Be sure the source is detailed enough to meet your needs and that it is written at an understandable level. A source written for elementary or high school students may be too simplistic; a source written for graduate students or professionals in a particular field may be too technical.

- Determine whether the author is expressing facts or opinions. Both are valuable, but facts must be verifiable, and opinions must be backed up with reasonable logic and evidence.

- Before using a website as your source, determine its accuracy and professionalism. Are there typos, dead links, and amateur graphics? If so, beware. Find out the site's sponsor. Sites sponsored by universities, news sources, or research foundations are usually credible. Those sponsored by hate groups, for-profit companies, and individuals with no expertise are suspect. Check when the site was last updated. Look at the links. Do they take you to credible sites?

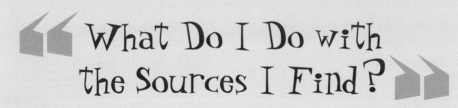

CHAPTER TWENTY-NINE

"What Do I Do with the Sources I Find?"

I f you used the strategies in Chapter 28, you found sources in the library and on the Internet—maybe you even found too many sources. After all, this is the Information Age, and you may be over-whelmed by the number of sources you found. Now you need strategies for determining which sources are useful to you and which you can eliminate. Then you must determine how to use those sources that *are* helpful. This chapter can help.

READ STRATEGICALLY

The following strategic reading strategies can help you determine quickly whether a source includes helpful information.

- If the source has a title, headings, or table of contents, skim them to determine whether relevant, useful information is included.
- If there is an index, look it over for indications of valuable content.
- If there are a preface, introduction, or chapter or unit summaries, skim them to determine whether your topic is touched upon.
- Read the first sentence or two of paragraphs in important chapters. For an article, read a sentence or two of each paragraph. If a particular paragraph looks promising, read all of it.
- Read the last paragraph of an article or relevant book chapters, looking for key ideas.
- Note boldface, italicized, and underlined terms and determine whether they are important to your topic.
- Consider pictures, graphs, and other illustrations for indications of usefulness.

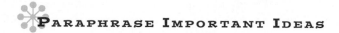

Paraphrase Important Ideas

To **paraphrase,** rewrite a useful idea in *your own words and style.*

- Do not add meaning that is not in the source.
- Do not change the author's meaning.
- Do not use the author's distinctive phrasings unless you put them in quotation marks.
- Do not rewrite by going word-by-word and substituting synonyms.

Source   The Bill & Melinda Gates Foundation, the richest in the country, is leading the philanthropic drive for small schools; it's committed more than $200 million to starting new ones nationwide or restructuring large high schools into smaller schools-within-a-school.

—Catherine Gewertz, "The Breakup: Suburbs Try Smaller High Schools," *Education Week*

Acceptable paraphrase   According to one author, the Bill & Melinda Gates Foundation has pledged over $200 million to building small high schools and also to reconfiguring existing large high schools to make them "smaller schools-within-a-school" (Gewertz).

The above paraphrase is <u>acceptable</u> for the following reasons:

- For the most part, the writer expresses Gewertz's ideas without using Gewertz's phrasings and style.
- When the writer *does* use Gewertz's exact words, they appear in quotation marks.

Unacceptable paraphrase   According to one author, the Bill & Melinda Gates Foundation, which is the wealthiest in the United States, is spearheading the charitable movement advocating small schools; the foundation has pledged more than $200 million to starting new small schools across the country or restructuring large high schools into smaller schools-within-a-school (Gewertz).

The above paraphrase is <u>unacceptable</u> for the following reasons:

- The writer merely substitutes synonyms. For example, "spearheading the charitable movement" is substituted for "leading the philanthropic drive."
- The writer does not use quotation marks to indicate the use of exact words, such as "restructuring large high schools into smaller schools-within-a-school."

Use Summary When Appropriate

When you want to give just the gist—the overall sense—of an author's ideas, write a **summary,** which is a highly condensed version of a source. A summary may express the ideas of several paragraphs in just a few sentences, or it may express the ideas of an entire article in just a paragraph or two. A summary restates an author's ideas in your own words and style, without changing or adding meaning.

Source   the preface of this book

Summary   According to its preface, *A Troubleshooting Guide for Writers* describes strategies to help writers develop good writing processes and solve writing problems. All of the book's features work to achieve those two goals.

Use Quotations Appropriately and Correctly

You can quote material that is difficult to paraphrase or that is expressed in a particularly effective way. Quotations should be punctuated according to the conventions explained in Chapter 24. When you quote, retain the wording, punctuation, spelling, and capitalization in the source, with the following exceptions.

To Omit Something from a Quotation

If you need to omit a letter, word, phrase, or sentence, use three spaced periods, called **ellipsis points** (. . .), to mark the omission. If the omission comes at the end of a sentence, add a period.

Source   The Bill & Melinda Gates Foundation, the richest in the country, is leading the philanthropic drive for small schools; it's committed more than $200 million to starting new ones nationwide or restructuring large high schools into smaller schools-within-a-school.

—Catherine Gewertz, "The Breakup: Suburbs Try Smaller High Schools," *Education Week*

Quotation   One researcher explains, "The Bill & Melinda Gates Foundation . . . is leading the philanthropic drive for small schools . . ." (Gewertz).

To Add Something to a Quotation

If you need to add something to a quotation to make it fit your sentence, or if you need to add an explanation, place the addition within **brackets** ([]).

Source   Circleville High School is one of 325 schools, most of them high schools, that the state has closed since 1990 in a push to consolidate small schools.

—Alan Richard, "School Merger Foes Rallying in West Virginia," *Education Week*

Quotation   According to *Education Week*, "Circleville High School is one of 325 schools, most of them high schools, that the state [West Virginia] has closed since 1990 in a push to consolidate small schools" (Richard).

To Quote Something That Already Includes a Quotation

If the source includes a quotation, use single quotation marks (') (') to designate this quotation within a quotation.

Source   "There is too much acceptance of mediocrity," said Michael L. Ward, the tall, soft-spoken superintendent of the West Clermont Local School District, which has 9,100 students.

—Catherine Gewertz, "The Breakup: Suburbs Try Smaller High Schools," *Education Week*

Quotation   One author says that according to school superintendent Michael L. Ward, "'There is too much acceptance of mediocrity'" (Gewertz).

To Introduce a Quotation with *That*

If you introduce the quotation with *that,* do not capitalize the first word (unless it is a proper noun), and do not use a comma after the introduction.

Source   The political winds around the issue may be shifting as well, with the impending retirement of a longtime legislative advocate of consolidation.

—Alan Richard, "School Merger Foes Rallying in West Virginia," *Education Week*

Quotation   One author notes that "the political winds around the issue may be shifting as well, with the impending retirement of a longtime legislative advocate of consolidation" (Richard).

Quotation   One author notes, "The political winds around the issue may be shifting as well, with the impending retirement of a longtime legislative advocate of consolidation" (Richard).

To Use a Lengthy Quotation

If your quotation runs more than four lines in your paper, you should indent the quotation rather than use quotation marks. Do not further indent the first word, even if it begins a paragraph in the source, unless you are quoting multiple paragraphs.

Source   Many free-speech controversies, especially on college campuses, are grounded in concerns for civility, politeness, and good taste. They also tend to follow the same path and end the same way. A government entity regulates speech in an effort to elevate discourse, limit the profane, and protect public and personal sensitivities; courts strike down the regulations as violating the First Amendment freedom of speech; and we end up right where we started.

—Howard M. Wasserman, "Fan Profanity," *Patterns for a Purpose*

Quotation   Howard Wasserman explains the cycle that free-speech debates often take:

> Many free-speech controversies, especially on college campuses, are grounded in concerns for civility, politeness, and good taste. They also tend to follow the same path and end the same way. A government entity regulates speech in an effort to elevate discourse, limit the profane, and protect public and personal sensitivities; courts strike down the regulations as violating the First Amendment freedom of speech; and we end up right where we started (633).

✳CONSIDER YOUR THESIS

Review the notes you took in light of your writing topic and thesis. Does the information in your notes suggest that you should rethink your thesis idea, perhaps because you learned something unexpected or did not confirm a point you hoped to confirm? If so, revise as necessary.

✳INCORPORATE YOUR NOTES INTO AN OUTLINE

When you outline your paper, be sure to indicate where you will incorporate the source material in your notes. As you outline, you may discover that some of your source material is not usable. You may also find that you need to rework your outline to use some of your notes.

✳INTEGRATE SOURCES WITH EACH OTHER AND WITH YOUR IDEAS

To **integrate** source material you must work it into your writing smoothly in one of the following ways:

- Include words that show how two or more paraphrases, summaries, or quotations relate to each other.
- Include words that show how source material relates to your own ideas.
- Include words that show how source material relates to a thesis or topic sentence idea.

Paragraph 2 of the sample paper on page 174 is a good example of integrating source material. In this paragraph, the writer combines paraphrase and quotation from two sources and shows how this source material relates to the thesis idea that school consolidation is a good idea. The source material supports the thesis idea by pointing out the advantages of school consolidation. The paragraph is given here, with the words that help integrate the source material underlined as a study aid.

Erik Nelson is among those who applaud the trend. He believes the strongest argument for school consolidation is that one large school is superior to multiple smaller ones because the large school can offer a greater variety of classes and extracurricular activities. He maintains that the larger enrollment makes it possible to provide a broader selection of courses, and that extracurricular offerings, including athletics, will thrive because of the merging of available monies (3). Barney Berlin and Robert Cienkus also see the advantage of consolidation. They explain in "Size: The Ultimate Educational Issue?" that "very small districts and schools seldom have the resources—equipment, consultants, ancillary staff, curriculum variety, supplies, teaching staff—to do as good a job as larger districts" (229).

Paragraph 8 of the sample paper is another good example of integrating source material. In this paragraph, the writer relates paraphrases from two sources to his own ideas to show that small schools have advantages, but those advantages are offset by their drawbacks. In the paragraph, which is reprinted here, the writer's own ideas are underlined as a study aid.

Certainly small schools also have important advantages. Small class sizes mean more individual attention, but that attention does not offset lack of exposure to diverse populations. Fewer students means more pupils can find places on athletic teams and in other extracurriculars, but that benefit is offset by the fact that the number and variety of those activities are limited. In a small school, the relationship between students and teachers can be closer, and, as Allan Ornstein reports in "School Size and Effectiveness: Policy Implications," pupils in smaller high schools tend to have higher scores on standardized tests (240). However, those benefits do not hold up in college if students in small schools tend to drop out. Furthermore, according to *Education Week*, it is unclear how the size of a school affects test scores because studies are inconclusive (Gewertz).

DOCUMENT SOURCE MATERIAL APPROPRIATELY

When you paraphrase and quote, you must acknowledge that you are using other people's ideas and words, and give credit to the original writer with correct **documentation.** You can ensure proper documentation by doing the following.

Follow the Appropriate Style Sheet

A **style sheet** is a guide to how to handle source material. Papers written in the humanities, including composition, usually follow the latest edition of the *MLA Handbook for Writers of Research Papers*—often called the MLA style sheet. Papers in many social sciences courses follow the latest edition of the *Publication Manual of the American Psychological Association*—often called the APA style sheet. You can find information on these two style sheets in your campus bookstore or online at http://owl.english.purdue.edu. Click on the link for the MLA Formatting and Style Guide or the APA Formatting and Style Guide, whichever you need. If you are unsure which style sheet to use, ask your instructor.

Introduce Source Material

Introduce each paraphrase and quotation with one or more of the following: the author's name, the author's credential, or the title of the source. In most cases, the verb should be in the present tense. Here are some examples:

- For example, Alan Richard says
- One researcher reports that
- According to *Scientific American,*
- As scientist Dick Grinstein writes in *Scientific American,*

Cite Your Source in Parentheses

If you are using the MLA style sheet, follow these guidelines:

- If the introduction to the paraphrase or quotation includes the author's name, place the page number the material came from in parentheses.

MLA EXAMPLE   Barney Berlin and Robert Cienkus explain that "very small districts and schools seldom have the resources—equipment, consultants, ancillary staff, curriculum variety, supplies, teaching staff—to do as good a job as larger districts" (229).

- If the introduction to the paraphrase or quotation does not include the author's name, place both the author and page number in parentheses.

MLA EXAMPLE   Two authors explain that "very small districts and schools seldom have the resources—equipment, consultants, ancillary staff, curriculum variety, supplies, teaching staff—to do as good a job as larger districts" (Berlin and Cienkus 229).

- For an online source when page numbers are not available, put the author's name in parentheses. If the author is not given, place the title in parentheses.

MLA EXAMPLE   As one author reports, "You can reduce your . . . cost by increasing the size of the [school] facility" (Fanning).

- If the source has three authors, list all three authors' last names with a comma between each and the word *and* before the last name.

MLA EXAMPLE   Some educators are convinced that consolidated schools are both educationally sound and fiscally responsible (Watkins, Richards, and Chu 90).

- If the source has more than three authors, give the first author's last name followed by *et al.* (*Et al.* is the Latin abbreviation for "and others." Note that no period appears after *et*, but one does appear after *al.*)

MLA EXAMPLE   On the other hand, a number of educators maintain that consolidated schools can overwhelm students and faculty (Jordan et al. 56).

- If you cite more than one work by the same author, include a shortened title for the work you are citing to identify it. Also include the author's name followed by a comma if the name is not mentioned in the introduction to the paraphrase or quotation.

MLA EXAMPLES   Gewertz maintains that test scores are not a reliable indication of how school size affects learning ("Size").

One researcher maintains that test scores are not a reliable indication of how school size affects learning (Gewertz, "Size").

NOTE: Page numbers do not appear in the previous two examples because the source was found online.

If you are using the APA style sheet, follow these guidelines:

- Place the publication date in parentheses.
- If the author's name is mentioned in the introduction to a paraphrase, follow that name with the year of publication in parentheses.

APA EXAMPLE   According to Nelson (1985), the strongest argument for school consolidation is that one large school is superior to multiple smaller ones because the large school can offer a greater variety of classes and extracurricular activities.

- If the author is not named in the introduction to a paraphrase, include the name and publication date in parentheses at the end of the paraphrase. Page numbers for paraphrases are encouraged, but they are not required. Notice the commas and the use of *p.* for the page number.

APA EXAMPLE   According to one author, the strongest argument for school consolidation is that one large school is superior to multiple smaller ones because the large school can offer a greater variety of classes and extracurricular activities (Nelson, 1985, p. 346).

- Include page numbers for quotations directly after each quotation. Notice the commas and the use of *p.* for the page number.

APA EXAMPLES   Barney Berlin and Robert Cienkus (1989) explain that "very small districts and schools seldom have the resources—equipment, consultants, ancillary staff, curriculum variety, supplies, teaching staff—to do as good a job as larger districts" (p. 229).

Two authors explain that "very small districts and schools seldom have the resources—equipment, consultants, ancillary staff, curriculum variety, supplies, teaching staff—to do as good a job as larger districts" (Berlin & Cienkus, 1989, p. 229).

- If the source has five or fewer authors, name all the authors the first time you mention the source in an introduction. Subsequent introductions can use the first author's name and *et al.*, unless there are only two authors. In that case, always use both names. Use *and* for multiple authors in the text and the ampersand (&) for multiple authors within parentheses.

APA EXAMPLES   According to Ellis, Rubin, and Strauss (2006), school consolidation has become a fiscal imperative in rural areas (p. 12).

According to some, school consolidation has become a fiscal imperative in rural areas (Ellis, Rubin, & Strauss, 2006, p. 12).

Include a List of Your Sources

For correct documentation, the last page or pages of your paper should list the sources from which you paraphrased and quoted. MLA guidelines call this list of sources the "Works Cited" page. APA guidelines call it "References." Both the works cited page and references page are an alphabetical listing according to the author's last name. If no author is given, the work is alphabetized by the first word in the title (excluding *A, An, The*). For an example of a list of sources written according to MLA guidelines, see page 177.

MLA Works Cited Forms: Print

Book by One Author

Richo, David. *The Five Things We Cannot Change and the Happiness We Find by Embracing Them*. Boston: Shambhala, 2005. Print.

Book by Two or Three Authors

Hallowell, Edward M., M.D., and John J. Ratey, M.D. *Answers to Distraction*. New York: Bantam, 1996. Print.

Book by More Than Three Authors

Davidson, James West, et al. *Nation of Nations: A Concise Narrative of the American Republic*. 4th ed. New York: McGraw-Hill, 2006. Print.

Book by an Unknown Author

Macmillan Science Library: *Genetics*. New York: Macmillan, 2002. Print.

Book Edition Other Than the First

Zinsser, William Knowlton. *On Writing Well: An Informal Guide to Writing Nonfiction*. 5th ed. New York: Harper, 1994. Print.

Book with an Editor

Winokur, Jon, ed. *Advice to Writers: A Compendium of Quotes, Anecdotes, and Writerly Wisdom from a Dazzling Array of Literary Lights*. New York: Random House, 2000. Print.

Book by an Author with an Editor

Arnold, Matthew. *Culture and Anarchy*. Ed. J. Dover Wilson. Cambridge: Cambridge UP, 1961. Print.

More Than One Book by the Same Author

Tannen, Deborah. *I Only Say This because I Love You: How the Way We Talk Can Make or Break Family Relationships throughout Our Lives*. New York: Random House, 2006. Print.
———. *You Just Don't Understand: Women and Men in Conversation*. New York: Ballantine, 1990. Print.

Selection from an Anthology

Smith, Hale. "Here I Stand." *Readings in Black American*
Music. Ed. Eileen Southern. New York: Norton, 1971.
286—289. Print.

One Volume in a Multivolume Work

Reich, Warren. *Encyclopedia of Bioethics*. Vol. 2. New York:
Macmillan, 1995. Print.

Encyclopedia Article

"Terrorism." *Encyclopaedia Britannica*. 11th ed. 2001. Print.

Article in a Weekly or Biweekly Magazine

Alter, Jonathan. "An Erosion of Trust." *Newsweek* 26 May
2003: 47. Print.

Article in a Monthly or Bimonthly Magazine

"Where to Invest Now." *Consumer Reports* Mar 2003: 34. Print.

Article in a Newspaper

El Nasser, Haya. "High-tech Bust Drains Bay Area Population."
USA Today 10 July 2003: A1. Print.

Article in a Scholarly Journal

Tong, T. K. "Temporary Absolutisms versus Hereditary
Autocracy." *Chinese Studies in History* 21.3 (1988):
3—22. Print.

MLA Works Cited Form: Portable Databases (CD-ROMs, Diskettes, and Magnetic Tapes)

"Real Facts about the Sun." *The Dynamic Sun*. Washington:
NASA, 2000. CD-ROM.

MLA Works Cited Forms: Online Sources

The MLA works cited forms for online sources generally look like this model.
Note that the first date is the publication date and the second date is the date of
access.

Goleman, Judith. "An 'Immensely Simplified Task': Form in
Modern Composition-Rhetoric." *Conference on College*
Composition and Communication. 56.1 (2004): 51—71.
Web. 12 Oct. 2004.

To write a works cited form for an online source, gather the information in the
following list when it is available:

- The author's and editor's names.
- The title of the work.
- The name of the online site.
- Publisher information.
- The date of electronic publication.
- The date you accessed the material.
- The electronic address (URL), printed between carets (< >) after the date of access, only if locating the source or website is difficult—that is, if the source cannot be located using a search engine or search box at the site.

Because online sources change often and lack a standardized format, it is not possible to come up with models that cover every instance. The forms below should cover most online sources. If you have a source that does not completely conform to one of these models, do the best you can to supply all the information your readers need to find the source themselves.

Scholarly Website

Bahri, Deepika, ed. *Postcolonial Studies*. Emory University, 13 Nov. 2002. Web. 1 Dec. 2008.

Part of a Scholarly Website

Ahmed, Aziza. "Victorian Women Travelers in the 19th Century." *Postcolonial Studies*. Ed. Deepika Bahri. Emory University, Fall 998. Web. 1 Dec. 2008.

Article in an Online Encyclopedia

"Abbott, Berenice." *Encyclopaedia Britannica Online*. Encyclopaedia Britannica, 2007. Web. 31 March 2008.

Article in an Online Journal

Woodruff, Eliot Ghofur. "Mertical Phase Shifts in Stravinsky's *The Rise of Spring*." *Music Theory Online* 12.1 (2006): n. pag. Web. 3 Apr. 2006.

NOTE: Use *n. pag.* if no page number is given.

Article from an Online Daily Magazine

Miller, Laura. "The Fall of Man." *Salon.com*. Salon, 20 May 2007. Web. 21 May 2007.

Article from an Online Weekly Magazine

Leo, John. "Self-Inflicted Wounds." *U.S. News and World Report*. U.S. News and World Report, 11 Oct. 2004. Web. 14 Oct. 2004.

Article from an Online Monthly Magazine

Quirk, Matthew. "How to Grow a Gang." *TheAtlantic.com*.
    Atlantic Monthly Group, May 2008. Web. 13 May 2008.

Article in an Online Newspaper

"Two More Records Fall on Day Two of League Championships."
    YSUSports.com. Department of Athletics, Youngstown
    State U, Youngstown, Ohio, n.d. Web. 19 May 2008.

NOTE: Use *n.d.* if no date of publication is given.

Blog Posting

Gladwell, Malcolm. "NBA Heuristics." Gladwell.com. 10 Mar. 2006.
    Web. 21 May 2006.

APA Reference Forms: Print

Book by One Author

Richo, D. (2005). *Five things we cannot change and the
    happiness we find by embracing them*. Boston, MA:
    Shambhala.

Book by Two Authors

Hallowell, E. M., & Ratey, J. J. (1996). *Answers to dis-
    traction*. New York, NY: Bantam Books.

Book by Three to Seven Authors

Davidson, J. W., Gienapp, W. E., Heyrman, C. L., Lytle,
    M. H., & Stoff, M. B. (2005). *Nation of nations: A
    narrative history of the American republic* (5th ed.).
    New York, NY: McGraw-Hill.

Book Edition Other Than the First

Zinsser, W. K. (1994). *On writing well: An informal guide
    to writing nonfiction* (5th ed.). New York, NY: Harper.

Book with an Editor

Winokur, J. (Ed.). (2000). *Advice to writers: A compendium
    of quotes, anecdotes, and writerly wisdom from a
    dazzling array of literary lights*. New York, NY:
    Random House.

Book by an Author with an Editor

Arnold, M. (1961). *Culture and anarchy* (J. D. Wilson, Ed.).
    Cambridge, England: Cambridge University Press.

Selection in an Anthology

Rubenstein, J. P. (1967). The effect of television violence on small children. In B. F. Kane (Ed.), *Television and juvenile psychological development* (pp. 112–134). New York: American Psychological Society.

Encyclopedia Article

Terrorism. In *Encyclopaedia Britannica* (Vol. 28, pp. 511–517). Chicago, IL: Encyclopaedia Britannica.

Article in a Weekly or Biweekly Magazine

Taibbi, M. (2009, July 9). The great American bubble machine. *Rolling Stone*, 1082, 52–61, 98–101.

Article in a Monthly or Bimonthly Magazine

Lethem, J. (2009, June). The American vicarious: Nathanael West's novels prophesied Ronald Reagan, reality TV, and other future domestic dilemmas. *The Believer*, 7(5), 3–6.

Article in a Newspaper

Powell, M. (2009, July 10). To get to Sotomayor's core, start in New York. *The New York Times*, pp. A1, A16.

Article in a Scholarly Journal with Continuous Pagination through Volumes

Hall, R. M. (2003). The "Oprahfication" of literacy: Reading "Oprah's book club." *College English*, 65, 646–667.

Article in a Scholarly Journal with Separate Pagination in Each Volume

Tong, T. K. (1988). Temporary absolutisms versus hereditary autocracy. *Chinese Studies in History*, 21(3), 3–22.

APA Reference Forms: Online Sources

To write a reference for an online source in APA style, keep the following in mind:

- In general, include the same information for online articles that you would include for print articles, including an issue number in parentheses.
- You need not include a retrieval date (date of access) for any content in its final form—such as articles from journals or *Time* magazine, for example. Do include a retrieval date for content likely to change, such as pages from websites, content from blogs, or material from wikis.
- Some journal articles will include a digital object identifier (DOI) on the first page. This is a numbered and lettered locator that provides a longer-lasting link than many URLs. When it is available, provide the DOI instead of the URL. When a print article includes a DOI, provide the DOI at the end of the reference.
- If you have an online source not covered by a model here, provide everything you think readers will need to locate the source on their own.

Article from an Online Magazine

Beam, C. (2009, July 13). What the president ordered. *Slate*.
  Retrieved from http://www.slate.com

Article from a Newspaper

Wade, N. (2008, July 31). Couch mouse to Mr. Mighty by
  pills alone. *The New York Times*. Retrieved from http://
  www.nytimes.com

Journal Article with DOI (Online or Print)

McCracken, H. (1989). Who is the celebrity endorser? Cultural foundations of the endorsement process. *European
  Journal of Marketing*, 16(3), 1125—1134. doi: 10.1086/
  209217

Journal Article with No DOI (Online)

Mead, G. H. (1925, April). The genesis of the self and
  social control. *International Journal of Ethics*, 35(3),
  251—277. Retrieved from http://www.jstor.org/pss/237727

Article on a Website

Watson, D. (2005, May 15). *Photosynthesis: How life keeps
  going*. Retrieved from http://www.ftexploring.com/
  photosyn/photosynth.html

Online Encyclopedia Article

Solar cell. (2001). *In The Columbia encyclopedia*. Retrieved
  from http://www.bartleby.com/br/65.html

Wiki Article

Homeopathy. (2009, June 10). *In Citizendium, The Citizens'
  Compendium*. Retrieved July 14, 2009, from http://en.
  citizendium.org/wiki/Homeopathy

Blog Posting

Gladwell, M. (2006, March 6). NBA Heuristics. Message posted
  to http://gladwell.typepad.com/gladwellcom/2006/03/nba_
  heuristics.html

PLAGIARISM ALERT

You will be guilty of **plagiarism** if you hand in all or part of another person's work as your own or if you use sources and fail to document them properly. To avoid plagiarism, which can have serious penalties, remember the following:

- Never turn in another student's work as your own, and never submit as your own all or part of a paper you have downloaded from the Internet.
- Do not copy and paste Internet material into your paper without using quotation marks or without paraphrasing or summarizing it.
- Use quotation marks when you include another writer's words.
- Quote accurately, using ellipsis points and brackets as needed.
- Never add or change meaning when you paraphrase or summarize.
- Introduce source material appropriately.
- Parenthetically cite the source for every paraphrase, quotation, and summary.
- Cite every source you use on a works cited or references page.

CHAPTER THIRTY

"What Does an Essay with Sources Look Like?"

I f you have never written or read an essay with sources, you may not be able to visualize such an essay or imagine yourself writing one. The following student essay, which uses sources, illustrates many of the points made in Chapters 28 and 29. These points are noted in the margins. Studying the essay, which follows the Modern Language Association (MLA) style sheet explained in Chapter 29, can help you better understand how writers can incorporate source material into their writing.

Edmund Parker

Professor Muller

English 550

17 December 2010

Heading
Title is centered.

Paragraph 1

A. The ellipsis points are for an omission in the quotation.

B. The bracket is for an addition to the quotation.

C. The parenthetical citation is for an electronic source.

D. The last sentence is the thesis.

Paragraph 2

Notice the synthesis of sources.

A. The second sentence begins a paraphrase. Notice it is introduced with a present tense verb.

B. The reintroduction helps the reader know that the paraphrase continues.

C. The parenthetical citation is a page number because the author's name appears in the introduction.

D. Notice the direct quotation.

Paragraph 3

A. The first sentence is the topic sentence.

B. Paraphrase and quotation are combined to support the topic sentence.

The Benefits of School Consolidation

1 In response to shrinking enrollments in some districts and a steady decline in funding for education, we are seeing more and more consolidation of schools because, as reported in "Rural School Consolidation and Student Learning," "You can reduce your … cost by increasing the size of the [school] facility" (Fanning). Even when funding and enrollment are not an issue, some schools are combining in an effort to improve the quality of education and use tax dollars more efficiently. While school consolidation has its critics, combining schools is both practical and educationally sound.

2 Erik Nelson is among those who applaud the trend. He believes the strongest argument for school consolidation is that one large school is superior to multiple smaller ones because the large school can offer a greater variety of classes and extracurricular activities. He maintains that the larger enrollment makes it possible to provide a broader selection of courses, and that extracurricular offerings, including athletics, will thrive because of the merging of available monies (3). Barney Berlin and Robert Cienkus also see the advantage of consolidation. They explain in "Size: The Ultimate Educational Issue?" that "very small districts and schools seldom have the resources—equipment, consultants, ancillary staff, curriculum variety, supplies, teaching staff—to do as good a job as larger districts" (229).

3 Some small school districts lack the tax base to build new schools or make necessary repairs to older buildings. For example, according to *Education Week*, Circleville High School in West Virginia had to be closed because the school desperately needed repairs and "local money wasn't an option," since the local tax base was too small to raise the needed funds (Richard).

Paragraph 4

This paragraph is developed with the writer's ideas.

Paragraph 5

This paragraph is developed with the writer's ideas.

Paragraph 6

A.–B. Notice that the introduction to the paraphrase is two sentences.

Paragraph 7

Notice that the writer's ideas are integrated with source material.

A.–B. The quotation and paraphrase support the topic sentence.

C. This sentence expresses the writer's own thinking.

Paragraph 8

Note the integration of sources with the writer's ideas.

⁴ In addition to providing academic and extracurricular enrichment, consolidated schools are better able than small ones to foster the emotional and social development of students. In small schools, students have a very restricted social setting, so they have few, if any, opportunities to interact with people from different social, ethnic, racial, and religious backgrounds. Some schools are so small that the students are with the same small group of classmates from first grade through graduation.

⁵ Lack of opportunity to interact with a diverse group is not the only social problem that exists in small schools. The size can also create identity problems. In a small school, a student is so well known by peers and teachers that he or she can become trapped in a certain identity, such as "athlete," "brain," or "dummy." The identity becomes hardened in the minds of students and teachers, making it difficult for the labeled student to break out of the role and engage in different activities.

⁶ Ⓐ While the small class size in small schools allows for individual attention, it can create problems for students later in college. Ⓑ Jane White addresses this issue. She writes that a guidance counselor at one small school feels that the adjustment from small classes to large college classes is so difficult for many students that they drop out of college (49–50).

⁷ The benefits that consolidation provides come at a cost savings overall. Ⓐ According to Nelson, "Expenditures for capital improvements and basic maintenance are reduced because there is no need to upgrade or maintain duplicate facilities." Ⓑ Nelson goes on to note that consolidated schools require fewer administrative personnel and teachers (3). Ⓒ Furthermore, while a small school may not be able to afford special staff such as reading specialists, special education instructors, and media specialists, a consolidated district with its larger budget may be able to hire these important professionals.

⁸ Certainly small schools also have important advantages. Small class sizes mean more individual attention, but that attention does not offset lack of exposure to diverse populations. Fewer students means more pupils can find places on athletic teams and in other extracurriculars, but

that benefit is offset by the fact that the number and variety of those activities are limited. In a small school, the relationship between students and teachers can be closer, and, as Allan Ornstein reports in "School Size and Effectiveness: Policy Implications," pupils in smaller high schools tend to have higher scores on standardized tests (240). However, those benefits do not hold up in college if students in small schools tend to drop out. Furthermore, according to *Education Week*, it is unclear how the size of a school affects test scores because studies are inconclusive (Gewertz).

Paragraph 9

The conclusion provides a strong finish by citing an authority.

[9] *Education Week* reports the findings of the superintendent of the Pendleton County schools in West Virginia on the advantages of consolidation. While the superintendent admits that the one-on-one attention available in small schools is lost, he notes that in consolidated schools students have more advanced math classes, they are around more students their own age, and "they can join a full-size band or choir" (Richard). All in all, school consolidation is a positive trend.

Works Cited

Berlin, Barney M., and Robert C. Cienkus. "Size: The Ultimate Educational Issue?" *Education and Urban Society* 21 (1989): 228–231. Print.

Fanning, Jim. "Rural School Consolidation and Student Learning." *ERIC Clearinghouse on Rural Education and Small Schools.* ERIC Digest, 1995. Web. 1 Dec. 2003.

Gewertz, Catherine. "The Breakup: Suburbs Try Smaller High Schools." *Education Week.* Education Week, 2 May 2001. Web. 30 Nov. 2003.

Nelson, Erik. "School Consolidation." *ERIC Digest.* ED 282346. Washington: Office of Educational Research and Improvement, 1985. Print.

Omstein, Allan C. "School Size and Effectiveness: Policy Implications." *The Urban Review* 22 (1990): 239–245. Print.

Richard, Alan. "School Merger Foes Rallying in West Virginia." *Education Week.* Education Week, 10 Apr. 2002. Web. 30 Nov. 2003.

White, Jane Robertson. "To Reorganize or Not Reorganize: A Study of Choice in a Small District." *ERIC Digest.* ED 28627. Ithaca: New York State College of Agriculture and Life Sciences at Cornell Univ, 1986. Print.

PART VI

Appendixes

APPENDIX A
"English Is Not My First Language."

APPENDIX B
"I Get Nervous Writing in Class and Taking Essay Examinations."

APPENDIX C
"I Need a Writing Topic."

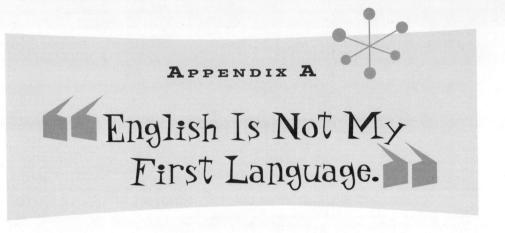

"English Is Not My First Language."

If English is your second or third language, you have richer cultural and linguistic resources than people who know only one language. Sure, you may struggle with written or spoken English from time to time—or perhaps you struggle often. But your struggle is only temporary, for eventually your facility with English will increase, especially if you use the strategies in this appendix. In the meantime, realize that you are way ahead of those who know only a single language—and realize that people who speak multiple languages can be excellent writers in all their languages.

LISTEN TO THE RADIO AND TELEVISION

The more you hear English, the faster you will internalize its grammar, vocabulary, and syntax. So listen to news radio while you are driving, and turn on the television while you are doing chores. Make note of words and structures you do not understand, and ask about them in your English class, the International Students office (if your campus has one), or the writing or tutoring center.

SPEAK UP

Don't let uncertainty about your English skills prevent you from talking in class or to native users. Instead, speak as often as you can. Ask questions and make comments in class; strike up conversations with native users. Then put a big smile on your face and invite people to correct your mistakes. Others will gladly help you, and you will improve faster.

BE PATIENT WITH YOURSELF

Recognize that language learning is a process played out over time. Mistakes are a natural and inescapable part of that process, so don't berate yourself for them. Instead, view your errors as learning opportunities, and be patient with yourself because time is on your side.

✳ KEEP A LIST OF IDIOMS

An **idiom** is an expression whose meaning cannot be understood from the definitions of its individual words. For example, the idiom "under the weather" means "not feeling well"—a meaning you cannot figure out by putting together the individual meanings of the words *under, the,* and *weather.* To learn idioms, keep a list of the ones you read and hear, along with their meanings. Study the list regularly. If you need to check a meaning, look up the key word in a large dictionary, and the idiom may be given. For example, you can find the meaning of "under the weather" by looking up *weather.*

To help you recognize idioms, here are five examples. If you do not know any of them, use them to begin your idiom study list.

1. across the board—applying to all instances or people

   Example: The insurance company is raising its premiums *across the board.*

2. to be in someone's shoes—to have the same experience as someone else

   Example: I would change roommates if *I were in Tazim's shoes.*

3. to have somebody in stitches—to make the person laugh very hard

   Example: The comedian's stories *had the audience in stitches.*

4. a lost cause—a hopeless case

   Example: You might as well give up looking for the contact lens in this clutter; it's *a lost cause.*

5. to pick up the tab—to pay the bill

   Example: You paid for lunch last week. I'll *pick up the tab* today.

✳ THINK IN ENGLISH

Think in English when you speak and write. If you think in your native language and then attempt to translate, you are more likely to have problems with sentence structure, vocabulary, and idioms.

✳ REMEMBER THAT AN ENGLISH SENTENCE MUST USUALLY HAVE BOTH A SUBJECT AND A VERB

Some languages do not require a stated subject, and some do not require a stated verb. English sentences, however, must have both a subject and a verb—except when the sentence issues an order, makes a request, or makes a suggestion. In that case, the subject need not be stated.

No (lacks a subject):	Was late for our appointment.
No (lacks a verb):	Juan late for our appointment.
Yes (has a subject and a verb):	Juan was late for our appointment.

Yes (issues an order):	Do not be late for our appointment.
Yes (makes a request):	Please do not be late for our appointment.
Yes (makes a suggestion):	Consider being early for your appointment.

✻ DO NOT ADD AN −S OR −ES TO THE SECOND VERB IN A TWO-WORD VERB

When the complete verb is composed of two verbs, do not add -s or -es to the last verb.

No:	The dog <u>can jumps</u> through a hoop.
Yes:	The dog <u>can jump</u> through a hoop.
Yes:	The dog <u>jumps</u> through a hoop.

✻ AVOID USING PRONOUNS TO REPEAT SUBJECTS AND ANTECEDENTS

1. In some languages, a pronoun can repeat the stated subject, but not in English.

No (*it* repeats *blouse):*	Mary's new blouse, it is silk.
Yes:	Mary's new blouse is silk.
Yes:	It is silk.

2. Do not use a pronoun to refer to an antecedent (noun that the pronoun stands in for) when that antecedent is already referred to by *who, which,* or *that.*

No (*which* already refers to bag so *it* is unnecessary):	Someone took my bag, which I left it on the desk.
Yes:	Someone took my bag, which I left on the desk.

✻ PAY ATTENTION TO COUNT AND NONCOUNT NOUNS

Count nouns name people, places, objects, emotions, or ideas that can be counted. They are words such as *child, city, wallet, fear,* and *concept.* **Noncount nouns** name things that cannot be counted. They are words such as *air, baggage, cereal, water,* and *honesty.*

1. Use a singular verb with noncount nouns.

No:	Our <u>baggage are</u> lost.
Yes:	Our <u>baggage is</u> lost.

2. Do not use *a* or *an* with noncount nouns.

No:	I feel <u>a pride</u> for what I accomplished this year.
Yes:	I feel <u>pride</u> for what I accomplished this year.

✳ KNOW WHEN TO USE A, AN, AND THE

1. Use *a* before words beginning with a consonant sound; use *an* before words beginning with a vowel sound.

   a turtle   *an* old turtle

   a concept   *an* interesting concept

   a hat   *an* awning

   U can sometimes have a consonant sound and sometimes have a vowel sound.

   a union   *an* umbrella

2. Use *a* when the letter *h* is pronounced and *an* when it is silent.

   a hurricane   *an* honorary degree

3. With singular count nouns, use *a* and *an* when their specific identity is unknown to the reader or listener, and use *the* when the identity is known.

   Miguel applied for <u>a</u> job.

   Miguel applied for <u>the</u> manager job at the recreation center.

   Do not use *a* or *an* with plural words.

   No: Miguel applied for <u>a</u> jobs.

   Yes: Miguel applied for jobs.

   Do not use *a* or *an* with noncount nouns.

   No: Lizette offered <u>an</u> advice.

   Yes: Lizette offered advice.

4. Use *the* to point out something specific.

   <u>The</u> mayor must work to attract new businesses. (This sentence refers to a specific mayor.)

   <u>A</u> mayor must work to attract new businesses. (This sentence refers to mayors in general.)

✳ KNOW WHEN TO USE IN, ON, AND AT

1. Use *in* for seasons, months, and years that do not include specific dates. Use *on* if a specific date appears.

   I got married <u>in</u> 2005.

   I got married <u>on</u> June 3, 2005.

2. Use *in* for a period of the day. Use *at* for a specific time of the day. Use *on* for a specific day.

   Carlotta swims laps <u>in</u> the afternoon.

   Carlotta swims laps <u>at</u> 1:00 each day.

   Carlotta swims laps <u>on</u> Tuesdays.

3. Use *in* for a location that is surrounded by something else. Use *at* for a specific location.

My apartment is <u>in</u> the middle of town.

Let's have dinner <u>in</u> the kitchen tonight.

My apartment is <u>at</u> 3033 Millroad Circle.

Meet me <u>at</u> the library to study.

Appendix B

"I Get Nervous Writing in Class and Taking Essay Examinations."

It's natural to feel nervous when you have to write in class or take an essay examination because in addition to writing credibly, you must write quickly. Fortunately, a certain amount of anxiety is helpful during timed writings because it keeps you alert and focused, thereby helping you to perform well. Thus, if you are nervous before or during a timed writing, do not be concerned. That said, too much anxiety can make you panicky and hurt your performance, so the trick is to keep the anxiety at the facilitating level. The strategies in this appendix will help you achieve that level.

PREPARE

No set of strategies can make up for failure to study for an exam or read assigned materials in anticipation of an in-class writing assignment. You can also prepare by writing and answering essay questions before the exam and by practicing writing essays in a limited amount of time.

REDUCE YOUR EXPECTATIONS

Recognize that timed writings will not be as strong as those produced in a more extended time frame, so reduce your expectations accordingly. And remember, in timed writing situations, information is more important than style.

VISUALIZE YOURSELF COMPLETING THE TIMED WRITING

Visualization is a great stress reducer. Repeatedly picture yourself in the classroom receiving the exam sheet or writing topic, reading it over, writing a scratch outline, drafting responses successfully, and feeling confident.

✳ USE AN ABBREVIATED VERSION OF YOUR WRITING PROCESS

The fact that you are writing against the clock does not mean you should skip steps in the writing process—just abbreviate them. Write a quick scratch outline, as explained below. Draft quickly from start to finish. Revise and edit directly on the page, making only the most crucial changes.

✳ BUDGET YOUR TIME AND WEAR A WATCH

Decide how much time you will spend on each question or how much time you will spend outlining, drafting, and revising. Base your decision on the amount of time you are given and the number of questions you are expected to complete or the length of the essay you are expected to write. For example, if you have one hour to answer four questions, plan to spend 15 minutes on each one. If some questions are worth more points than others, spend the most time on the questions worth the most points. Of course, you will have to keep track of the time, so wear a watch.

✳ ORGANIZE SIMPLY

Time is not on your side, so forget elaborate introductions and conclusions. Open with a thesis that reflects the exam question or assigned topic and go on to make your points. For example, if the question is "Explain manifest destiny," begin this way: "Manifest destiny is . . ." If the writing topic is "Discuss the positive aspects of competition," you might begin this way: "Competition's chief advantage is that it facilitates progress and creativity."

✳ PREPARE A SCRATCH OUTLINE

Jot down the main points you want to make and then number those points in the order you plan to write about them. This scratch outline will keep you organized and thereby minimize your stress.

✳ DO NOT START OVER OR RECOPY

Keep to the plan you set up with your scratch outline because you do not have time to start over. Nor do you have time to recopy, because rewriting takes valuable time away from drafting, revising, and editing—and builds in opportunity for error. Write legibly, but don't worry about being perfectly neat. Cross-outs and arrows are acceptable, as long as your instructor can easily follow along.

Write on Every Other Line or Leave Generous Margins

The extra space will make it easier to add material that occurs to you during revising.

Never Pad Your Writing

Your instructor will recognize the irrelevant material and likely be annoyed by it. You do not want to annoy the person giving you a grade.

If You Do Not Know an Answer, Take a Reasonable Guess

If you are lucky, you may get some points. Guessing is not the same as padding, however. Keep your answer to the point.

If You Run Out of Time, List the Points You Would Have Included

You may get partial credit if you demonstrate your knowledge.

Look for Direction Words

Look for direction words like the following; they will tell you the kind of information your instructor is looking for.

analyze: Break into separate parts and give the characteristics of each part.

compare: Show the similarities between two or more items.

contrast: Show the differences between two or more items.

define: Give the meaning of a term or concept.

describe: Give the characteristics, features, and important qualities.

discuss: Consider or argue the merits or pros and cons of an issue; give a detailed account of an issue or concept.

evaluate or interpret: Give your opinion of the significance of something.

illustrate: Explain by giving examples.

If You Do Not Understand a Question or an Assignment, Ask for Clarification

You may not get help, but then again, you may.

APPENDIX C

"I Need a Writing Topic."

Sometimes you get to choose your own topic for an essay or journal entry. You may be excited to have this freedom—you may even have just the right topic in mind. Or you may be overwhelmed—there's just too much choice, and you can't decide. In the latter case, try one of the topics given in this appendix.

1. The student services division of your university plans to publish a handbook for first-year students to familiarize them with important procedures. As a student employee in student services, you have been asked to contribute to the handbook by writing an essay that explains how to do one of the following:

   a. Get a student ID.

   b. Register for courses.

   c. Select a suitable adviser.

   d. Rush a fraternity or sorority.

   e. Manage stress.

   f. Prepare for final examinations.

   g. Find a compatible roommate.

   h. Select a major.

   When you write the essay, remember that your audience will be new students, and your purpose will be to inform them so that they are better able to cope with campus life.

2. Campus administration is concerned about drinking at your university. You are president of student government and have been asked to help prepare an alcohol policy aimed at reducing underage drinking and promoting responsible drinking among those of legal age who choose to drink. You can include ideas for regulations, education, disciplinary policies, and anything else you care to address. Your audience is university administrators, and your purpose is to help develop a policy to reduce unsafe and illegal drinking practices on your campus and to persuade administrators to adopt your ideas.

3. A big birthday bash is being planned for someone you respect and care a great deal for (pick anyone you regard highly—a friend, a relative, a teacher, a coach, a member of the clergy). You have been asked to write a character sketch of the person that presents and illustrates one or two of the person's best traits. Mention the trait or traits and go on to give examples that illustrate the trait(s). The sketch will be reprinted as a party favor. Your audience is people who also know and care for the person, and your purpose is to praise the person.

4. You are a member of the local Chamber of Commerce, which is putting together a brochure to promote area tourism. Pick a spot in your area (a recreational spot, a historic area, an educational place, an amusement park) and write a description of it to be included in the brochure. Your audience is the traveler looking for a place to spend some time, and your purpose is to persuade the person to visit your area.

5. For the past week you have been home with the flu, and to pass the time you have watched television. The programming aimed at children, you have noticed, is unsatisfactory: The shows and commercials are manipulative, aimed at getting children to pester their parents for toys and sugared food. Write a letter of protest to the networks to persuade them to improve the quality of shows and commercials aimed at children.

6. When you were in high school, you were the editor of the school newspaper. Now your alma mater is planning a press day, and you have been asked to deliver a speech that expresses whether or not high school principals should be permitted to censor the contents of high school publications. Your audience will be the newspaper and yearbook staffs; your purpose will be to convince your audience.

7. Congratulations! You are the winner of a writing contest. Your prize is the opportunity to have a 700-word essay published in the magazine of your choice. You may write on any topic and for any purpose. Just be sure your material is suitable for the readers of whatever magazine you choose.

8. As a guest columnist for your campus newspaper, you plan to write an article about an important campus issue, such as diversity, grading policies, degree requirements, or extracurricular programs. Your audience is the campus community, and your goal is to convince readers.

9. You have recently begun an e-mail correspondence with someone who lives in another country. That person has asked you to describe American life as honestly and precisely as possible. Pick one aspect, such as shopping, dating, college life, high school, or presidential politics, and write an explanation for someone who knows very little about this country. Your purpose is to inform.

10. Pick a controversial issue and write a letter to the editor of your town newspaper expressing your opinion on the issue. Your audience is the

readers of the newspaper, and your purpose is to persuade them to think or act in accordance with your opinion.

11. You are a member of the local school board. Recently, a number of parents have complained because commencement ceremonies traditionally begin with a nondenominational prayer. Although no particular religion is represented by the prayer, these parents maintain that any prayer is inappropriate because it violates the separation of church and state guaranteed by the Constitution. Furthermore, these parents maintain that the rights of atheists are violated by the prayer. Do you agree with these parents? Write a position paper that either recommends abolishing the prayer or recommends retaining it, and support your assertion. Your audience is the rest of the school board, and your purpose is to convince them to take the course of action you recommend.

12. As part of a job application, you must write a character sketch of yourself that presents and illustrates your chief strengths and weaknesses. Your audience is the personnel director, and your purpose is to present a realistic yet favorable portrait.

13. If you have a job, assume that your boss has asked you to write a report that explains one change that could be made to improve efficiency, morale, or profitability. You should explain the change, why it is needed, and how it would improve operations. Your audience is your boss, and your purpose is to persuade this person to institute the change.

14. In a study skills class, your instructor has assigned a paper that requires you to classify and describe the study habits of students. To research this paper, interview as many students as necessary to discover how they study, how much they study, when they study, and where they study. Your audience is your instructor, and your purpose is to inform.

15. You are taking a psychology course, and to help you appreciate how people are affected by events in their lives, your instructor has asked you to write an essay that explains how some event in your life has affected you (a death, a divorce, making a game-winning touchdown, being cut from a team, being class president, failing a test, moving to a new town, and so on). Your audience is your instructor, and your purpose is to gain insight into the effect of an event.

Index

✳ USE A REVISING CHECKLIST

A revising checklist, like the following one, keeps you from overlooking some of the revision concerns. In addition, you can combine this checklist with reader response by asking a reliable reader to apply the checklist to your draft. You can also save it as a computer file to consult each time you revise. (The page numbers in parentheses refer to helpful pages in this book.)

Content

1. Does your writing have a clear thesis that accurately presents your focus? (page 31)
2. Does every point in your writing clearly relate to that thesis? (page 14)
3. Are all your generalizations, including your thesis, adequately supported? (pages 13–14)
4. Are all your points well suited to your audience and purpose? (pages 6 and 8)
5. Have you avoided stating the obvious? (page 95)
6. Does your introduction create interest in your topic? (page 48)
7. Does your conclusion provide a satisfying ending? (page 60)

Organization

1. Do your ideas follow logically one to the next? (pages 14–15)
2. Do your paragraphs follow logically one to the next? (pages 14–15)
3. Do the details in each paragraph relate to the topic sentence? (page 14)
4. Have you used transitions to show how ideas relate to each other? (page 84)

Expression

1. When you read your work aloud, does everything sound all right? (page 71)
2. Have you avoided wordiness? (page 91)
3. Have you eliminated clichés (overworked expressions)? (page 94)
4. Have you used specific words? (page 93)
5. Did you use a variety of sentence openers? (page 97)
6. Have you used the active voice? (page 94)
7. Have you used action verbs rather than forms of *to be?* (page 94)
8. Have you used parallel structures? (page 99)